CW00493226

BUSTED

Celebrating
30 Years of Publishing
in India

BUSTED

DEBUNKING MANAGEMENT MYTHS WITH LOGIC, EXPERIENCE AND CURIOSITY

ASHOK SOOTA

PETER DE JAGER

SANDHYA MENDONCA

HARPER
BUSINESS

An Imprint of HarperCollins *Publishers*

First published in India by Harper Business 2023
An imprint of HarperCollins *Publishers*
4th Floor, Tower A, Building No. 10, DLF Cyber City,
DLF Phase II, Gurugram, Haryana – 122002
www.harpercollins.co.in

2 4 6 8 10 9 7 5 3 1

P-ISBN: 978-93-5699-321-1
E-ISBN: 978-93-5699-325-9

Typeset in 11.5/15.2 Aldine401 BT at
Manipal Technologies Limited, Manipal

Printed and bound at
Manipal Technologies Limited, Manipal

This book is produced from independently certified FSC® paper to ensure responsible forest management.

Dedicated to the curious, hopeful and self-motivated readers who seek to build value for themselves and their organizations

Contents

Part 3
Busting Myths about People and Organizations

Preface

How does a statement almost become a universal truth or what we describe as a myth? This happens because more often than not, it holds a degree of truth.

If the statement has been said from an acknowledged management guru, then, inevitably, a flood of articles and essays follow, until it becomes a widespread, oft-repeated, unquestionable, accepted truth. Take, for example, the following from Michael Porter—the essence of strategy is choosing what *not* to do—or from Peter Drucker, who is reputed to have said, 'culture eats strategy for breakfast'.[1]

We acknowledge that there is a core of truth in these statements, and it is not our aim to question the wisdom of these management greats. Yet, statements are deceptive if other angles are not perceived, or other points of view are not examined.

These concise statements from respected mentors currently not in the room with us offer huge value in helping us analyse the challenges we face, enable focused thinking and act as guidelines for us to follow. The problem occurs when they replace well-considered contemplation and become a way to abdicate our responsibility of the decision-making process.

This phenomenon isn't restricted to the professional sphere; it is part of the human condition. Consider the following well-known epigrams:

Look before you leap.
vs
He who hesitates is lost.

And this pair:

You are never too old to learn.
vs
You cannot teach an old dog new tricks.

And this one:

It is better to be safe than sorry.
vs
Nothing ventured, nothing gained.

Each of these has proven and historical value, or else we would not repeat them. Each is true based on our personal experiences and the experiences of others. We can all tell stories that highlight, reinforce and perpetuate the wisdom of each of these observations. Yet, we cannot deny that they contradict each other.

While we find this ambiguity somewhat amusing, we recognize that the context in which we find ourselves tells us which of these we should follow in a particular situation.

The problem occurs when such adages dominate all our decisions. This doesn't happen often with these more mundane types of sayings, but it's not uncommon for it to happen in our professional spheres. Who dares contradict an observation made by a management guru when publication after publication repeats it? That's our objective in this little tome—to challenge, tickle and poke at a handful of those accepted, the unassailable 'professional truths'.

Let's examine Michael Porter's statement first. There is no doubt that strategy requires constant and prolonged focus, and demands that we learn to say 'no' to new ideas, to protect us from a world of possible distractions. The flip side: errors of omission get detected too late and are far more expensive than errors of commission. When Bill Gates was asked what his biggest mistake or failure was, he responded: 'Not developing Android'. Here was the world leader in operating systems (OS), acknowledging that he didn't expand his strategic vision to do what was needed to compete effectively, let alone dominate, in the exploding OS market for mobiles.

His response points to an important lesson, if we're willing to recognize and apply it to our processes. If we allow a strategy we've used in the past to determine everything we are going to do—or not do—in the future, then we've placed too much confidence in our younger, less-informed selves. In an evolving market, we cannot afford to shackle ourselves to our historic strategic vision.

Furthermore, the concept of broadening our market presence is undergoing a massive change, partly due to the convergence of technologies. Microsoft, therefore, entered the search domain with Bing, while Google expanded into operating systems. Both forayed into hardware with their mobile phones. Google and many others entered the world of online payment systems through Google Pay, competing with other payment apps such as BHIM, Paytm, PhonePe and the like.

We have an even bigger objection to the aforementioned statement by Michael Porter. But what after we have said no? Perhaps, many years later, we'll discover an error of omission.

After we've said 'yes', there would be so much to be done to ensure successful execution of the strategy, including branding and positioning of our product or service, market segmentation, and pricing for each segment. We need to figure out our go-to market approaches, increasingly involving technology platforms and social media and all the while watch the competition, including emerging competition, and proactively or reactively respond to changes.

Regarding our view on 'culture eats strategy for breakfast', we invite you to read our essay within. We must add here that we revere Peter Drucker, and we also see the core truth in what he is reputed to have said.

Some of the myths are downright deceptive and erroneous. Take, for example, the mantra that we are 'over-led and under-managed'. We firmly believe leadership and management are two sides of the same coin, and both an excellent leader and an excellent manager are important for sustained success. Trying to place one above the other can lead to bad results, as you will see in the following essay.

Some of the myths owe their origins to erroneous assumptions about people. For example, the belief that people resist change draws on a fallacious model whereby leaders introduce changes while the rank and file resist them. We believe the reverse is true: people welcome change. This includes changes in strategy, positioning, processes, policies and organizational structure. People instinctively perceive that change is the key factor for remaining ahead. Of course, some changes may appear to create losers along with winners. How we address this loss—whether perceived or real—is what will determine the success of the change.

Some myths are overly simplistic, such as people leave people, not organizations. This reflects a perception that bosses are toxic, like the pointy-haired boss of the Dilbert comic strip. The strip should be seen as what it is—a comic strip. However, it does spread cynicism.

The supporters of this myth ignore the complexity of building organizations, the challenges of meeting all aspirations, and the challenges of retaining people in a world where demand for certain skills has become sky-high—as is the case with all digital skills today.

Here's another example. Organizations are unique and complicated, exist in different stages of growth and decline, operate under different financial rules and government-imposed constraints, tap into different technological ecosystems and transact with wildly different customer bases. Yet, we talk about best practices, as if it's possible for any solution to apply across this wide ocean of variety and produce similar results. Even a cursory examination of that idea should have us questioning this approach to solutions.

Ideas, and especially short, pithy soundbites, can go viral and take on a life of their own. It takes a certain type of courage to point out a flaw or a weakness in a statement accepted by nearly everyone else. Just search any of the topics within this book on the internet and you will be amazed by the tons of articles espousing these and, fortunately, quite a few also opposing them. Unfortunately, many of these myths give you a unidimensional, and at times erroneous, view of what makes the world tick.

The essays within this book acknowledge what's real and true, but also give you the opposite and a more balanced view of what makes the world tick. We hope you enjoy reading this book, and that it will widen your horizons!

Presenting both sides of that discussion has proven more enjoyable than we anticipated. Unsurprisingly, we—Ashok and Peter—don't always agree completely, and that itself is part of the lesson. The validity of any of these management myths is influenced greatly by our personal experiences. Sandhya Mendonca, our collaborator for this book, added to the discussion by digging deeper and questioning us. She also spoke to industry practitioners Nandan Nilekani, T.T. Jagannathan, Sandeep Maini, Manish Sabharwal, Hema Ravichandar, Revathy Ashok and academician Rishikesha Krishnan about these dictums. Their views add a great deal of value to the book.

The mistake is in assuming that these management dictums are always true or false in all circumstances. The purpose of this book is simple: we are inviting the reader, perhaps even challenging the reader, to join us in thinking deeper about the things we might otherwise accept at face value.

Have fun and enjoy the debate.

Ashok and Peter

Part I

Busting Myths about Strategy

1

Culture Eats Strategy for Breakfast

ASHOK SOOTA

'Culture eats strategy for breakfast' is attributed to Peter Drucker. No one is sure if Drucker really said this, and it does not appear in any one of his thirty-nine books. It was popularized by Mark Fields, president of Ford, who believed in it passionately. Like all myths, this statement acquired followers who went overboard to propagate it further. Like Torben Rick, a business-improvement and change management specialist, says 'organizational culture eats strategy for breakfast, lunch and dinner, so don't leave it unattended'.[1]

In recent years, we have witnessed the adverse impact of negative cultures in high-profile companies, such as poor governance in Enron and Satyam Computers. The male-dominated macho culture or 'brotopia',[2] which predominated in Uber till the advent of Dara Khosrowshahi, is also prevalent in many Silicon Valley companies. Thus, it's not surprising that interest in the belief 'culture eats strategy for breakfast' has revived. Later in this essay, we examine what we opine are 'good' examples set by Azim Premji (Wipro), John Chambers (Cisco) and Nandan Nilekani (Infosys).

Differing Roles

Let's spell out the important, yet differing, roles of culture and strategy. Strategy focuses on what your business does and where you want to take it, while culture focuses on the 'how' and 'why' of operations. Make no mistake, we believe culture is extremely important. Companies with great cultures perform better and have longer business cycles. 'Companies with strong culture achieve three times higher total return to shareholders than others,' note Alexander DiLeonardo, Ran Li Phelps and Brooke Weddle in their article for McKinsey.[3]

There are many other studies that show such correlations, but there is a danger in such studies. It would be like saying that the sun rises because the rooster crows. Of course, the sun rises when the rooster crows, but it doesn't mean that the rooster's crowing led to the sunrise. Studies will certainly prove the positive correlation, but if a company is really successful, it also probably has a great culture and a great strategy.

We just believe that questions like 'strategy or culture: which is more important?' are false dichotomies. Another false question that propagates the myth is 'would you compromise culture for strategy?' You would no more do this than consciously choose a strategy that is not in harmony with your culture. An organization needs to continuously strengthen its culture and develop winning strategies. Quite definitely, we don't agree with the statement that 'culture eats strategy for breakfast'.

Culture is amorphous and difficult to measure. Peter, in a fascinating analogy of a Bonsai tree, describes it as follows:

'What we see at any specific time in an organization isn't really culture; it's the end product of a tremendous amount of activity in the form of mostly unconscious effort throughout the entire organization.' Culture is also the most important long-term differentiator for an organization—unique and not easy to replicate.

Strategy, on the other hand, requires a refresh every few years to develop new differentiators, as the original USP gets limited and products tend to get commoditized. This does not make strategy less important. Torben Rick also goes on to state that 'given strategy is typically viewed from a three-to-five-year time horizon and refreshed every few years, capabilities and culture also need to be reviewed at the same time and as one process'. We couldn't disagree more with this statement. Culture, in fact, needs to be reviewed and monitored continuously, since even a positive culture can turn toxic. When this happens, corrective action has to be initiated immediately; you can't wait for two-to-three-year cycles.

Building Trust

Culture is also like 'trust'. It takes years to build trust, but a single negative act can destroy it. Culture is difficult to assess and measure. We believe that an organization's foundation for culture depends on its values. If they are carefully thought-out, these values should stand the test of time. Culture and values determine behaviour, and that influences results. It is not enough to just articulate the values of the company. It is important to internalize them and live by them.

Happiest Minds's values are represented by the acronym SMILES, denoting sharing, mindful, integrity, learning, excellence and social responsibility. All team members, including Ashok, are assessed on whether they demonstrate these values. The culture needs to be reinforced by rituals, stories, reward and recognition systems, and continuous feedback. At Wipro, for well over twenty years, Azim Premji addressed all new employees on the beliefs of the company. These were two-hour interactive sessions where examples from the organization's history brought home the message that these beliefs translated into practices where leadership and management walked the talk.

The best example that I can cite is the culture of customer-centricity that John Chambers ingrained in Cisco.[4] Chambers served as Cisco's CEO from 1995 to 2015, and executive chairman from 2015 to 2017. I distinctly remember attending Cisco's annual convention for customers one year, and being impressed by the fact that Chambers was present at all networking sessions, including at breakfast. He didn't disappear after his speech in the morning, as CEOs customarily do, but stayed on to interact with the delegates whenever possible. When I had the opportunity to speak with him one-to-one, Chambers asked what he could do to help my company, and I told him we could certainly use his help. Chambers's recommendation helped Happiest Minds get Cisco as a customer.

Compare this with the culture set by Scott McNealy, the co-founder, chairman and CEO of Sun Microsystems. I remember that at an interaction I was invited to, along with other industry leaders, we were made to stand in the four corners of a large hall. McNealy was ushered in like a demi-god and spoke briefly to each group before exiting!

Many traditional Indian companies have not bothered to build or foster the right culture. To take a generalized view, they have either been too feudal and have centralized power, or have been lax in financial governance. Founders or owners did not see anything wrong in taking a slice of the deal for themselves when they ordered capital equipment. It was the nature of things in those days.

A more modern and transparent approach began with a fresh breed of companies in newer industries such as information technology (IT) in the 1990s. With their exposure to global corporate culture and intent of complying with them, these companies—such as Wipro, TCS and Infosys—set about creating a transparent and robust work culture.

We spoke with Nandan Nilekani, co-founder and non-executive chairman of Infosys, to substantiate this view. He said:

> I think there's no doubt that the IT companies that began in India brought in a new culture of transparent corporate governance and so on. And there were many reasons for that. One is that many IT companies were set up by first-generation entrepreneurs. The backgrounds of people at Infosys, led by Narayan Murthy and others, were not entrepreneurial. Murthy's father was a schoolteacher. My father was a mill manager. Raghavan's father was a lighthouse keeper. We came from very different backgrounds.

He emphasized:

> Because we are first-generation entrepreneurs and because a lot of our business was globally oriented, we wanted a company rooted in ethics, values, respect for everybody, putting the professional in front, and so on. And that is true of many companies. In a way, we were differentiating ourselves, saying that we represent a different ethos, we represent professionalism, we represent quality, we represent transparency. I think

> what you [Ashok] did first with MindTree and then with Happiest Minds is an example of a professional entrepreneur. What distinguishes these entrepreneurs is that firstly they believe in professionalism.

At Happiest Minds, we consider the Great Place to Work surveys to be among the best tools to assess organizational culture. Apart from the questions which lead to a measurable Trust Index, the survey also includes an exhaustive culture audit. Internal surveys are important, but not enough. Thus, an independent and external measure is a better validation of a company's culture.

Never has culture been more important than now. Organizations are grappling with adapting to new ways of life and work, and culture is being transformed. But there is the danger that a culture mismatch can defeat a well-thought-through strategy. I remember that while leading MindTree, a high-end IT services company, I was instrumental in acquiring a product company whose primary activity was the design of mobile phones for Kyocera. The product company team infuriated the parent company team by looking down on them as doing inferior work. The anger was amplified since the profits and cash flows of the services company were the sources of funding for the product design work undertaken in the merged entity. Whatever the other merits, it was an acquisition doomed to failure. Yet, this was not culture 'eating' strategy but a culture mismatch-defeating strategy.

Strategy Is Important

Lest our strong belief in the importance of culture has given you the impression that we believe it is more important than strategy, let's now turn to the importance of strategy. In what follows, whenever we use the term strategist, we are referring to CEOs and their teams of advisors, who are collectively responsible for their organizations' strategy.

We believe that strategy is the single most important function for the sustained and profitable growth of a company, continued competitive advantage and value creation for its stakeholders. In our essay on 'the essence of strategy is choosing what not to do', we have mentioned some aspects of strategy including its applicability during different stages of the life of a company.

Technology is bringing about a rapid convergence of industries; for example, telecom, media and entertainment. Many industries are being disrupted by technology, such as the growth of fintech, healthtech, edutech and retail through e-commerce. The role of the strategist is to be aware of where new competition is coming from; to continue to provide new differentiators for your business and even to disrupt your own business before others do the same. This requires foresight, the ability to look ahead and visualize the future landscape and shifting consumer preferences. This entails the generation of new ideas. There is also a need to understand the organization's key competencies and build on the strengths provided by it. The strategist needs to see both the forest and the trees, and even the dim distant horizon.

Tough Challenge

The challenge is getting tougher by the day, since the pace of change is accelerating. It took the internet fifteen years to move from Internet 1.0, the read-only version, to Internet 5.0, the semantic, interactive version. Today, we have many more new technologies, all of which are evolving rapidly. Strategies can create entirely new business models. These include the metaverse, 5G+, artificial intelligence (AI), machine learning, blockchain, robotic process automation (RPA), robotics and augmented and virtual reality (AR/VR), to mention only a few. The strategist needs to understand the possibilities these technologies create for your business, and also the threat they can create.

In today's world, there are platforms that lend themselves to multiple businesses. They enable you to make money while you sleep. They enable you to get into many segments that you could not do before. Take the example of Amazon, which possibly has twenty business lines under the same platform. Market pressures require you to review your major businesses every three to four years. Your businesses might be doing well, but they tend to plateau after a while if the strategy is not continuously refreshed.

The strategist also has to continuously create the future through innovation and entry of new business lines, for example. Reliance Industries Limited (RIL) does a very good job of this and has entered into completely unrelated industries.[5] But it was Reliance's Jio, the world's cheapest telecom service provider, that became a game-changer for the industry. It also became the world's fastest-growing telecom firm. Digital services, retail, media and entertainment are part of RIL's thriving ecosystem of modern businesses. These are powering the company through rapid technological changes and consumer shifts.

But before you rush headlong to diversify, a word of caution while reviewing your strategy. You must strive for a fine balance between biting off more than you can chew, and not being ambitious enough. Sometimes when unexpected changes catch you off-guard, an organization can go into decline. At this stage, the strategist moves to prevent a rapid downward spiral.

Most importantly, the strategist must see how to convert a problem into an opportunity. The strategist must make decisions on when to raise capital—ideally when the organization can do so rather than when it's desperately needed. The strategist must decide on the mergers and acquisitions (M&A) strategy while looking for acquisition targets that are both a strategic and cultural fit. Strategic decisions must also take into account the organization's capabilities to execute the strategy. Gaps in capabilities must be identified upfront, and actions taken to fill these, be it training for new roles, or hiring external persons. We can see from the above that strategy is a critical function.

To sum up in the words of Nilekani, whom we regard as a master strategist: 'Strategy is a little more dynamic in its nature, whereas culture is time-invariant. Both have a role to play. Culture is very important and is what keeps the company going through decades. It's the value system that is inherited and passed on as a generation of leaders changes. Proper culture becomes fertile ground to implement the right strategy. If you don't have it, no amount of strategy is going to make a difference.'

Whatever enterprise he takes up, whether it's in Infosys or elsewhere, Nilekani's first focus is on making sure that the organization is in the right place, with the right people, values, mission, goals, team effort, and collaboration. 'This is a big part of what I try to do. Once those building blocks are in place, you can always create a strategy. Strategy is also equally important. But the strategy will change based on where you are in your journey and the market reality,' he says.

From all of Peter Drucker's writings, it is evident that he saw both culture and strategy as critical to an organization's success. We believe that he never actually said that culture eats strategy, or one is more important than the other, and the statement has been erroneously attributed to him. We wish the reader great success in creating a high-achievement, high-caring culture, and strategies that ensure sustained success.

Key Takeaways

- Great culture and dynamic strategies are both prerequisites for an organization to succeed.
- A dynamic strategy seeks to future-proof an organization.
- A great culture provides the foundation for this.

2

The Essence of Strategy Is Choosing What Not to Do

Ashok Soota

Coming from a person of Michael Porter's stature, there has to be a core truth that perpetuated this myth. Certainly, there is a need to focus and not try to be all things to all people. 'Essence of strategy is choosing what not to do' is a clarion call for it.

The lack of focus, or the inability to say no, is best illustrated by the downfall of Kingfisher Airlines and Vijay Mallya, the entrepreneur behind it. Kingfisher was created as India's premier full-service airline. As you entered a Kingfisher plane, you were greeted by a video of Vijay Mallya welcoming you as a guest to his home. Business-class travellers were personally escorted by elegant ladies from check-in, past security, and to the departure gate. Very much like the treatment for premium guests in five-star hotels in India! Things couldn't be better for

Kingfisher, as it gained market share through its reputation for excellent service. Then a terrible thing happened. Vijay Mallya didn't say 'no'.

An opportunity was presented to Kingfisher to acquire India's largest budget carrier—the cash-strapped, loss-making Deccan Aviation. The grandiose vision of becoming India's largest airline prompted Mallya to clinch the deal. A year later, his own airline went bust. When Kingfisher realized that it didn't have enough cash to keep all planes running, multiple flights were cancelled abruptly. This created shock and disgust in the minds of consumers, leading to a sharp downward spiral. Another strategic blunder was to pile on debt to fund the acquisition. Mallya should have said 'no' to at least some of the debt and 'yes' to equity. This example is to show that we don't disagree with Michael Porter on the importance of saying 'no' sometimes, or many times, but we do disagree with him that it is the essence of strategy.

Errors of Omission

Errors of omission are far costlier than errors of commission, in terms of the opportunity cost. This, in effect, means consciously or otherwise saying 'no' when we should have pursued the opportunity.

When Bill Gates was asked what was his greatest mistake ever, he said not coming up with Android.[1] Here was the king of operating systems acknowledging that he hadn't seen the power shift towards mobile phones, where Google would become the dominant force. At least Gates could recognize his strategic error in hindsight; most of us don't know the cost of our errors of omission or our opportunity costs of saying 'no'.

Where we strongly disagree with Porter is his assertion that strategic choices will not result in a sustainable advantage if they lack meaningful trade-offs. These trade-offs occur when 'more of one thing necessitates less of another'; that is, to say 'yes' to a new project means you also need to say 'no' to another, or at least postpone it. If you don't, the implication is that the chosen project will be denied resources to make it a success. While this may be perfectly valid for Porter's Southwest Airlines example, it is by no means a universal truth. Even Porter's well-known and highly erudite 'five forces that shape industry competition' does not refer to the need for such trade-offs.

We believe one of the most effective strategists of the last century was Jack Welch. He defined strategy simply as being only in those businesses where General Electric (GE) could be in the top two or three in the world. This did not prevent him from saying 'yes' to many opportunities, leading to a diverse conglomerate that spanned from aircraft engines through high-end medical equipment to lighting and many more, including GE Capital, which once contributed more than half of its profits. This diversity in the business portfolio would have shocked the purists, who emphasized focus. Also, a deeper look at many of the businesses would indicate that most were highly diversified, and this variety was allowed as long as they met the strategic goal of being in the top three in their industry.

Changing Focus

The world and the times have changed, as also the concept of focus. Organizations are entering territories that have been dominated by other players. For example, Google's entry into operating systems with Android and Microsoft's into search with Bing. Such forays seem to strengthen the defence against one's own crown jewels. An organization like LinkedIn, itself a Microsoft company, began as a social media connector for business links. It now embraces talent acquisition and learning, both radically different businesses.

Google—directly and through its parent company, Alphabet—has entered into multiple businesses including Google Cloud, Google Pay, self-driving cars and life sciences, to name only a few. These diversifications (or acts of saying 'yes') have enabled Microsoft and Google to remain in the top-five of firms in terms of market capitalization.

Rapid changes in technology and the introduction of newer technologies like the cloud, artificial intelligence, robotic process automation and blockchain are disrupting many industries and making new businesses possible. Could Uber or autonomous vehicles have existed without these technologies? Furthermore, many new hi-tech businesses are now run off platforms that can digest and analyse big data, and also enhance the power of the platform through machine learning. These platforms help you make money while you sleep, enabling many new strategic choices to be made as your organization's ability to manage more diverse choices increases. Also, Application Programming Interfaces (APIs) built on these platforms enable organizations to address new businesses or newer market segments.

Our further grouse against Porter is what do you do after you have said 'no'? Do you track the opportunity loss? After you have said 'yes', there's still so much more to be done to say you have created a successful strategy. This includes a variety of sub-strategies: sourcing, financing, marketing, sales and channel, scale-up, and even an exit strategy. The importance of all these strategies is discussed a bit more in-depth in the chapter 'Culture Eats Strategy for Breakfast'.

The Right Choice

Strategy is about choice because you want to provide some value to a particular set of customers, which is significantly greater than what others are able to do, according to Rishikesha Krishnan, an expert in strategy, professor and director of the Indian Institute of Management, Bangalore. 'It's very unlikely, therefore, that you can do this simultaneously in multiple areas to multiple sets of customers,' Krishnan explained in a chat with us.

Krishnan added that Porter and others have popularized that focus is helpful, and when formulating strategy, 'it's important to be clear about the boundaries in which you will work, and you should certainly be clear about what you will not do, to avoid getting into a whole set of areas for which you don't have the right capabilities'.

He cited the example of the Larsen & Toubro (L&T) conglomerate, which exited several businesses it had ventured into—such as cement, electronics, and medical instruments—and retained the focus on its core strengths of complex engineering and large construction projects. Other companies are also increasingly quite clear that in the long run, there are certain kinds of businesses that are better suited to their capabilities, and they restrict themselves to those.

Diversification

Krishnan pointed out that there is a stream of thought which actually argues for greater diversification, and this justifies the existence of diversified business groups, like the Tata Group, which are into a wide variety of businesses. There is validity for a business like Tata, especially in a market like India, as many of the sectors in which it operates are perhaps not very well-developed and efficient. Therefore, Tata is able to come up with its own capabilities that overcome the deficiencies of those markets. For example, if one considers the labour market, traditionally, there have been challenges in finding high-quality managers. The Tata Group, because of its brand reputation, attracts superior managerial talent, which it is able to apply across a wide variety of industries. Similarly, another market that sometimes doesn't function very efficiently in India is the market for capital. Here again, Tata has an advantage for similar reasons and is able to attract significantly higher amounts of capital at a lower cost than others are able to, enabling it to go into a wide variety of industries.

An interesting aspect of the debate about diversification is historical perspective. When the Indian economy was liberalized in the 1990s and global players entered many verticals, there was a higher level of competition. Indian companies needed to be much more focused on the few things they did well in order to succeed, and most consulting firms advised Indian companies and business groups to narrow their portfolio and concentrate on the businesses in which they had some historical advantage.

The contrary view held that liberalization and subsequent opening up of the economy also offered many new opportunities. For example, the telecom sector presented a hitherto-closed opportunity, and some companies chose to enter it and went on to do well, while some didn't. There is varying reasoning at play, but the one thing in which the management research literature shows convergence is that ultimately what really matters is the kind of capabilities that a company has. If the nature of the capabilities is such that they have wide applicability across a range of sectors, then such companies can afford to be more diversified. This logic would be apt for the Tatas; most of their capabilities, like management or raising capital, have applications across multiple sectors, and this justifies going into more diversification.

IT Diversification

In the 1980s, software giant Infosys got into manufacturing. It set up two companies—Infosys Digital Systems, which made telex machines, and Infosys Manufacturing Systems, to make computer numerical control (CNC) machines. Neither worked, and Infosys shut them down because it realized that it was essentially a software culture organization. The company knew how to write, build, deploy and sell software, whereas manufacturing companies need a factory, electronics and a different kind of quality control and sales. This was alien to Infosys; it realized that at its core, it is a software company, and has stuck to it.

However, a company that has narrower capabilities, such as one that is good at a particular technology, may need to focus on that technology rather than going very far away into other areas in which it lacks competence or expertise. Information technology and IT services companies have diversified a little, but with some caution. Wipro, TCS and Infosys moved outside IT services into business process outsourcing (BPO), to a degree because they saw BPO as a similar business. It required moderate to highly complex IT implementation projects, which need large numbers of programmers, diverse skillsets, high levels of project management and quality management skills, and in which they could create value by delivering a very complex solution to a customer in a reasonable time at low cost.

Many of the customers for BPO were very similar to the customers who were already giving them software projects, and the two things could sometimes be combined so that they first built the software and then went on to continue working with the customer to implement it or use it with customers. But these IT services companies did not go far beyond technology-driven services, and for the most part, have chosen to stick to what they understand well.

Nandan Nilekani agreed that 'a lot of strategy is choosing not what to do'. 'We are spoiled for choice today. The world looks like an oyster and people have access to lots of capital. It's very enticing when every day somebody comes up with a great new idea. I think self-discipline is very important. The self-discipline of being very choosy about what you do and being very choosy about what you don't do,' he said to us on this topic.

'Good leadership is being able to sift through the ideas that come, and obviously back the right ones which fit into your larger game plan, but otherwise, be ruthless about not doing the things that you don't want,' he underlined.

'The other part about strategy is also not about choosing to do A or B. It is about building an environment where you can basically do A or B. In other words, optionality in strategy is very important. You have to create more flexibility and optionality in your strategy because the world is highly uncertain, and you can't predict where it's going,' he added.

The views of Nilekani and Krishnan provide many perspectives to the issue of focused strategy versus diversification. Krishnan's argument on why the Tatas got into so many industries while Indian industry was maturing is perfectly valid. However, today's diversification of the Tatas is largely driven by the explosion of opportunities in the digital world. The Tata Group, under the leadership of N. Chandrasekaran and with the tacit support of Ratan Tata, is building a portfolio of digital properties. I believe that through this strategy of diversification, Chandra is creating new entities which will become the future stars of the Tata Group when some of the current stars fade away.

Are we saying that we discard Porter's dictum entirely? Of course not. It remains relevant in current times. We could conclude that the essence of strategy is a combination of all the strategies that we have discussed and directed towards creating a profitable enterprise. This does involve saying 'no' to many opportunities but also saying 'yes' to several. Each opportunity is to be evaluated on its own merits, and those that will deliver sustained stakeholder returns need to be pursued.

Key Takeaways

- Today's digital world offers opportunities to enter many industries, and changes the concept under which Michael Porter's dictum was defined.
- Entry into new business does not require a trade-off; you don't have to say 'no' to other opportunities.
- The cost of errors of omission is higher than the errors of commission. The latter can be rectified, or course-corrected. In the former, you don't even know what opportunity you have lost.

3

It's Lonely at the Top

Ashok Soota

'Loneliness of command' is a phenomenon on which reams have been written, and there seems to be a copious amount of content that perpetuates the image of the lonely and isolated boss. Barring one time, which was a singular exception in my career, in the forty-five years that I have been CEO of several companies, I haven't felt that my job is lonely. This instance when I did feel lonely happened when I decided to leave MindTree. Still, there were plenty of other reasons to restore my sense of positivity and avoid loneliness. I will amplify this point later in this chapter.

First, let's understand what a CEO's role should be. I see it as leading the way towards creating a great organization with the highest standards of governance, building a great place to work, having highly satisfied customers and delivering excellent business results. Equally important is developing leaders at the next levels, to realize their potential. If a leader genuinely thinks of and acts towards his team as his family, then again there can be no feeling of loneliness. If a leader can sincerely accomplish some of the above, there is no question of being lonely. In fact, far from being lonely, I have experienced a glow of warmth, affection, pride and gratitude from the teams I have led, and this has continued for decades.

Let's examine why people say it's lonely at the top. It's largely because the CEO is regarded as the person running the company, and the feeling is that the buck stops with them. Undoubtedly, the CEO is held responsible for a company's failures, but they also get a lot of undeserved credit for its success. The leader has to accept that there would be many people responsible for success, and should not claim a disproportionate share of the credit. What's important is that the leader owns or shares the responsibility for any failure. Regardless of who else might have been part of it, in the end, it is one person who takes the decision. There could be people who might not have supported that decision, or perhaps there could be some who did not voice their concerns for some reason and went along with the decision. In the end, it's the CEO's responsibility. That's the major reason why people say that it's lonely at the top.

This reasoning also rests on the premise of the 'boss-subordinate' prism. It assumes that there is a gap in the relationship between the CEO and the rest. This gap creates loneliness. It is assumed that if a CEO is capable, they would ensure there is no crisis in the business, no cash pressure and such. But problems have a way of cropping up in unexpected ways, and could have unforeseen results.

I emphasize that the key to avoiding or overcoming the feeling of loneliness is to be always in touch with the team. It's important to communicate with them regularly and transparently, to let them know what you stand for and what the organization stands for. This is where the mission, vision and values that you have articulated come into play. I make it a point to run sessions with every new group of employees, to drive home these essentials and encourage the next rung of leadership to do the same. I'm certain that this helps build a warm rapport that would avoid or quickly dispel the feeling of loneliness.

Let's see why the myth of the lonely leader is commonly accepted. 'The phrase "it's lonely at the top" sounds clichéd, but for many top executives, it is a harsh reality,' says Manfred F. R. Kets de Vries, management scholar, psychoanalyst, and INSEAD Distinguished Clinical Professor of Leadership Development and Organizational Change.[1]

'A CEO's responsibilities tend to come with sleepless nights and constant worry about having made the right decisions. The psychological pressure can inflict an emotional strain that most employees will never experience. Outwardly, this may present as aloofness, which, in turn, makes it even harder for a CEO to remain effective, he elaborates.

Citing a survey in the *Harvard Business Review*, Thomas J. Saporito, an expert in CEO succession,[2] says that 'half of the CEOs report experiencing feelings of loneliness in their role, and of this group, 61 per cent believe it hinders their performance'. He adds that first-time CEOs are particularly susceptible to this isolation, and nearly 70 per cent of those who experience loneliness report that the feelings negatively affect their performance.

An entire industry thrives on the premise that being a leader or a boss is isolating; there are umpteen offers of leadership coaching and counselling to overcome this challenge. The global leadership-training industry is approximately 350–400 billion US dollars![3] Equally startling is what a *Forbes* article states, citing data provided by McKinsey, about the leadership industry. 'Most of these leadership programs fail to create desired results',[4] it says.

'It's lonely at the top' is a myth that we would like to bust. Let's begin with the selective reporting that perpetuates the image of a lonely leader. Much has been made of Tim Cook's words that his job as the CEO of Apple was 'lonely'.[5] But as Cook went on to say, 'I'm not looking for any sympathy; CEOs don't need any sympathy'. This sentiment is acknowledged by Laura Empson, professor at Bayes Business School. 'If you think it's lonely at the top, you are not doing it right,' she says.[6]

Some others decry the myth of lonely leaders. Business consultant Marion M. Chamberlain believes that 'it's lonely at the top' is one of the biggest leadership myths.

A true leader knows the importance of having people who support them and taps into the power of connections, according to Chamberlain. 'If leadership is approached from the right attitude, it sure isn't lonely at the top', she says.[7]

Contrary to the belief that power implies isolation, management professors Adam Waytz, Eileen Chou, Joe Magee, and Adam Galinsky contend that 'behavioral science research has demonstrated that power confers psychological resources on its holders that might help stave off the loneliness that can accompany isolation'. In an article titled 'Not Lonely at the Top' in *The New York Times*, they write, 'studies have found that power enhances power-holders' beliefs that they control their own fates, buffers them from stress and creates the perception that others are consistently "in their corner"'.[8]

This is borne out by Roger Schwarz in his book *Smart Leaders, Smarter Teams: How You and Your Team Get Unstuck to Get Results*.[9] Schwarz says leaders should overcome the 'unilateral control mindset' which leads to unilateral leadership. To my mind, this would create a sense of isolation of the leader. It could perhaps be remedied if one were to adopt what Schwarz describes as 'a mutual learning mindset' where you achieve your goals by learning from and with others. 'This means you're open to being influenced by others at the same time you seek to influence others. You see each member of your team having a piece of the puzzle. Your job, along with the other team members, is to jointly put the puzzle together. You view leadership as power with others, not over others, so you look for ways of sharing it. With a mutual learning mindset, power is not zero-sum. If you share power with others, you don't lose any yourself,' he writes.

One should note that gratitude has great value in building relationships. This is a key point that I emphasized at Happiest Minds—to express gratitude towards the team and their families for all that they do to make the company a success. In turn, gratitude comes back to you in abundant measure.

Earlier, I referred to the period when I was the chairman of MindTree. An incomprehensible incident (it remains so to me even now) occurred, which made me feel not just isolated but alienated from many of the co-founders. The feeling was saddening because I thought of them as my family. And indeed, so did they. They all openly acknowledged that the company would not have survived the dotcom bust without my leadership. I went through both pain and hurt over several months. There was loneliness that I had irrevocably lost this part of my family. And yet I was not alone. In parallel, I had the support of my family and dear friends, with whom I shared the incident and my pain. Within minutes of a conversation with two of the co-founders, I decided I would leave and start something afresh. With this came the realization that my MindTree family extended well beyond the handful of founders. This was borne out when I announced my new venture, Happiest Minds. I received hundreds of applications to join; these numbers were way beyond my capacity to absorb! The flow of the people from MindTree to Happiest Minds continued for years, up to today.

Though not germane to the aspect of loneliness, let me complete the MindTree story. First, it worked out for the greater good of all concerned. The leaders who succeeded me got their own place in the sun (until MindTree got acquired!), and I got a new runway for my entrepreneurial career at Happiest Minds. Within two years, at age seventy, I would have retired anyway, as per retirement rules for board members at MindTree. Strangely enough, my moving away ensured we remained friends, though no longer family. Finally, my decision to start Happiest Minds turned out to be the best decision I took for my business career. The record success of the IPO led me to create SKAN, a medical research trust. This, in turn, led to the idea of Happiest Health.

What would be of immense help in times of crisis is a supportive network: family, friends, peer group, and yes, perhaps, a coach. Apple CEO Tim Cook has talked about the importance of seeking out advice; he's turned to Warren Buffett for business advice, and Anderson Cooper for guidance before disclosing that he was gay.[10]

This is emphasized by Manfred F.R. Kets de Vries,[11] who offers it among other suggestions as a cure for the loneliness of command:

- Be aware and mentally prepared
- Build an external network of support
- Express gratitude

We spoke with Sandeep Maini, chairman of the Maini Group, a motor vehicle design and manufacturing entity, who's grown into the role of the chairman of his family-founded and family-run business. He said heading a family business ensures that he's not lonely because he's really not alone at the top. Maini and his two younger brothers regard each other as equals. What helps the three of them is the independent board their father had instituted, even though most small companies didn't have one. Outside of themselves, the brothers regard the board as a good peer group with whom they brainstorm. Sandeep Maini's family, the board and a good circle of friends have ensured that he's not lonely at the top.

However, he does not deny that there are a number of corporate leaders who feel lonely at the top; he believes instead of keeping these feelings bottled up, they can overcome them by seeking out trusted people and sharing their vulnerabilities.

Apart from family and friends, Maini affirms the value of networking with peers in the industry; he says he has become a much better version of himself by being part of various industry bodies. Discussions with and support from peers have added tremendous value, and he encourages everyone to join such groups.

If and when you are beset by loneliness, leadership expert Silvia Pencak suggests you use the time to 'evaluate your strengths and redefine your priorities, and invest in your own growth and improvement'.[12]

The coauthor of this book, Peter de Jager, sums it up as 'you will not be lonely if you were a leader that relied on the people you have hired. On the other hand, if your management style is autocratic and you don't confer with your top people, you would create a lonely place for yourself. Put more bluntly, loneliness at the top is self-imposed isolation'.

John Maxwell says in his book *Leadership Gold: Lessons I Have Learned from a Lifetime of Leading*[13] that 'loneliness is not a leadership issue … [it] is not a positional issue; it is a personality issue'. People can be lonely at the top, the middle or at the bottom of the rung. A great leader would never say 'it's lonely at the top'. 'If you are leading others and you're lonely, then you're not doing it right. Think about it. If you're all alone, that means nobody is following you. And if nobody is following you, you're not really leading!'

Key Takeaways

- Far from being lonely at the top, a leader can experience warmth, affection, love, pride and gratitude from the team.
- In turn, you must do what is the best possible for the development of the team and reciprocate the gratitude.
- You won't be lonely if you also have a family to lean on and a network you can turn to for support and advice.

4

Fail Fast, Fail Cheap

ASHOK SOOTA

Michael Jordan once said 'I have failed many times, but I have never gone into a game expecting myself to fail'.[1] Failures are inevitable, but I much prefer Jordan's approach—it's as applicable to a basketball game as it's to business.

One of the weirdest myths we have come across is 'fail fast, fail cheap'. As other people build on the original myth, it becomes even weirder. We have even seen this myth extended to 'fail fast, fail cheap and fail often'.[2] We could go even further and be less charitable by describing these statements as being more than a little bit 'misguided'.

Thought processes like these lead to thinking small, and prevent the entrepreneur from thinking big. Apart from that, can you visualize the damage to your reputation if you fail often and visibly so? These myths can create a self-fulfilling prophecy of failure, with the consolation that 'at least, we failed cheap'!

The emphasis should not be on failing at all. The goal should be to uncover and fix errors as early as possible so that they don't end up being too expensive. Instead of failing cheap, companies should adopt the strategy of fixing cheap. We agree that the more time it takes to discover a flaw, the more expensive it will be. However, stalling in the design phase and holding back the launch of the product is not the best way to go.

The reasoning behind the fail-fast viewpoint is that it gives you an opportunity to build prototypes, modify your product or service and test your strategies before you make big investments. This is not an approach for failing fast, but an essential approach for success in this agile, competitive world. You don't wait till your full product is ready, but make your release in stages as you complete your offering. Those who wait too long may find a competitor has swept the market.

Especially with new concepts and unproven ideas, it is of prime importance to enter the market as quickly as possible. Novel ideas need to be tested, tweaked and modified based on the reaction of the market. Don't devote a lot of time to designing the product, launching it, assessing the reception it receives, modifying it and relaunching it. As LinkedIn co-founder Reid Hoffman says, 'if you're not embarrassed by your first product release, you released it too late'.[3]

Sandeep Maini admits that the Maini Group has faced the adverse effects of delaying a product in order to perfect it. 'It's happened to us many times. There have been times when we have taken inordinate time to bring out a beautiful product. And while the end product has been very good, it was late, and we lost the first-mover advantage. The machine was dated because someone else probably beat us to it. If we had taken quick decisions and brought out a machine that was 80 per cent all right and put it out in the market, we would have known much faster if the machine was a failure and worked on fixing it faster. That has been a learning for us,' he said in conversations with us for this book.

He advised that 'fail fast, fail cheap' should not be taken literally. 'Be it while making Reva EV, India's first electric car, or any of our other products, we are making new stuff every day. Every decision costs money. One needs to know whether the idea or the innovation is going to work, whether it's in your go-to-market strategy or the technical aspect of the product, or whether it works well with your customer—anything you need to know quickly before you really put in large monies,' Maini said.

The company's practice is to set a deadline for measurable outcomes and take a call on the results. 'Before we start on a project, we check whether the timeline required for the project matches with the market expectation, and whether we can do it. Second, we put a very strict budget. Sometimes entrepreneurs tend not to put any budget for dream projects. If we can't bring out a product within a budget and time-frame, we drop it. It's important that the decision is based on certain characteristics and fundamental outcomes that can be assessed. And there have been many times that we had an idea that did not work and failed in what we wanted to achieve. Having a deadline has helped us save time and money. Whether a company is in design, manufacturing or service, it's cheaper to know if a project is going to work or fail, much faster, he highlighted.

The 'fail fast' brigade doesn't realize that the majority of the investments needed in creating a successful business are the costs of building an organization, creating distribution channels, setting up technology and logistic infrastructures, and building a brand. The cost of building the product or service would seldom exceed even 20 per cent of the total investments required. Furthermore, you may develop a perfectly good prototype or product, and yet, it may not succeed as the entrepreneur finds it difficult to scale.

Many research studies show that the inability to fund growth and the shortage of cash are among the top-two reasons for business failure. The fundamental reason for this is that most entrepreneurs don't even have an idea how much cash would be required before the business achieves cash break-even.

I have seen and advised about a hundred young entrepreneurs on their business plans. Most come with projections showing less than one million US dollars cash as their requirement, and yet the business plan projects generating profits that are multiple times that amount in the second or third year. My advice to them is to be realistic in estimating their funding requirements till the business reaches the point of cash break-even. They also need to have a mental map of the funding rounds that would be needed to reach that point. If not, they will run out of cash and fail.

Hike Messenger, India's answer to Facebook-owned WhatsApp, shut down in 2021 due to a lack of focus on profitability, among other reasons.[4] Only in 2020 did monetization start to come under the company's radar of goals. Five years since launch, Hike gained barely any revenue, let alone profits. During the same period, WhatsApp grew on a scale that was difficult to match.[5] Hike tried to launch new elements and failed. Its employee count grew from 140 to 380 in 2017, only to be cut down to 120 in a year, in an attempt to reboot.[6] The layoffs followed its realization that diversification had been a mistake.

Initially envisioned as a WeChat-like super-app, Hike had to scale down and unbundle the app into multiple apps. Experts believed that India was not ready for a super-app, since users were still in the formative stages of being app dependent, unlike Japan or China.[7]

It is important for companies to learn from the failures of their predecessors, before deciding to fail fast for themselves. Companies will have to abandon the fail fast-fail cheap approach as they grow and begin to succeed, because launching a new product could damage their brand equity.[8]

Another argument of the proponents of 'fail fast' is that after tweaking your product or service, you may need to implement a pivoting strategy. They ignore that a new pivoting strategy will also require cash, and probably not be cheap or inexpensive to implement. In 1999, when the dot-com bust happened, MindTree (I was the founding chairman and managing director from 1999 to 2011) was one of the few hundred internet system integrators globally that survived, and went on to do a very successful IPO. This was done by what Erik Ries, author of The Lean Startup book series, would have called a zoom-out strategy. We developed new offerings and services to enlarge our market address.

MindTree was able to do this because it had raised a fair amount of cash at inception, and supplemented it with the cash generated during the dot-com boom. On launch, MindTree had rushed into the market even while it was developing its offerings. If we had waited to test, modify and tweak before launch, we would have entirely missed the opportunity.

Mark Zuckerberg, who launched one of the biggest social media networks on the planet, also follows the motto 'move fast and break things'.[9] Before exploring and launching other social network ideas, a young Zuckerberg created ZuckNet, a platform for him and his sisters to communicate with their dad; and for their dad, who had a dental office, to communicate and share data with his co-workers across rooms.

This was a predecessor to the many ideas he would go on to explore. Unlike Hike Messenger, Facebook regularly tests out new ideas, and has created a constant feedback loop. There are probably 10,000 running versions of Facebook at any given point in time. Engineers can test new ideas by launching them to a select audience. After this, they go on to analyse how this new element affected all metrics. This system allows Facebook to test its assumptions, and also gives engineers the opportunity to move and test quicker, without having to go through layers of management. It is precisely the 'move fast, break things' strategy that has helped Facebook to scale fast. Creating a tight feedback loop with real products and real customers is one of the most effective ways to build a great product.

Another aspect of 'fail fast, fail cheap' is the impact on the team. If team members sense that the entrepreneur's philosophy or approach is to fail fast, fail early and fail cheap, they will probably bail out. People want to be part of a winning venture, where they also share in wealth creation. In fact, if this intent is stated even to potential new joiners, the entrepreneur will not be able to attract talent.

Apart from bootstrapped and angel-funded ventures, the largest source of start-up funding is from venture capitalists (VCs). Though all VCs will want an entrepreneur to spend prudently, we have never come across a VC who has advocated 'fail fast, fail early'. These VCs also are aware that maximum investment will be needed to scale the business, and that is where the risk levels also escalate. In these situations, they are also ready to put in large additional amounts, as evident from the money poured into entities like Uber, Airbnb, OYO and many e-commerce players. They know that they are in these ventures for the long run, and not with a view to fail fast, early and cheap. Also, VCs are aware that the enormous returns from the top 10 per cent of their ventures will compensate adequately for their loss-making ones.

We have to ask what it is that makes an entrepreneur successful while others fail. We believe it is qualities like resilience, and determination to succeed. We see 'fail fast, fail cheap' as a cop-out. Instead, we would say 'fight long, fight hard, fight smart and win handsomely'.

Peter offers a quote by Stephen McCranie that's relevant to the discussion: 'The master has failed more times than the beginner has even tried.'[10] Peter says that organizations must not let fear of failure stop them from entering new territory; such trepidation stifles innovation and growth. Obviously. And if things go wrong, organizations must also not be afraid of admitting they've made a mistake and changing their course of action. This is the 'sunk cost fallacy' that we discuss later in this essay, and this cost is not obvious to many.

The difficulty is balancing those two. Changing course every time a problem is encountered is a road to disaster, and staying with a problem too long, throwing good money after bad, is a different road to the same destination. This road is travelled more often than the first.

The 'Observe, Orient, Decide, Act' (OODA) loop concept is worth tapping into. It is a four-step methodology for decision-making that basically says:

1. See what is happening as a consequence of your actions, and how the environment is responding to those actions.

2. Adjust your view of how you might proceed, based on what you've observed.
3. Decide what your next action, a course correction if you will, should be.
4. Implement that action and then repeat the process.

Another visual image that might work well is that of the 'crow's nest' from the early days of sailing. A person in the crow's nest can see much further than those on deck, and can call for small course corrections long before the need to change course becomes a crisis. If the lookout sees rocks ahead, they can call for a small course correction of five degrees to starboard, far in advance of a possible crisis. Those on deck can then take their time to make the correction. This is not a 'fail cheap' strategy; it's 'fix cheap'.

If there was no one looking from the height of the crow's nest, by the time the people on deck would become aware of the danger, they might have to turn thirty degrees to starboard very quickly in order to avoid the rocks. This correction is not a 'fail cheap' event, it's a 'fail painfully' crisis.

The challenge, of course, in the advice we're offering is that 'fail fast, fail cheap' is focusing on failure, while 'fail fast, fix cheap' is really focusing on 'decide and act fast, and be ready to make constant course corrections'. This can avoid the tendency to get locked into old actions now proven wrong, that lead us into the sunk cost fallacy.[11]

This refers to one's tendency to see an endeavour through because we have invested heavily in it, even when it would be more beneficial to abandon the project. The best-known example of this fallacy is the decision to continue to build the supersonic plane, Concorde, even after it became clear that it would overrun the estimated cost of a hundred million US dollars.

While the sunk cost could not have been recovered either way, as a result of not abandoning the project, millions more dollars were wasted, and the plane operated for less than thirty years. Political compulsions seemed to have prevailed over the financial sense of the governments of the United Kingdom and France, but this is not a risk that commercial organizations can afford to take.[11]

On the other hand, persistence pays off when the situation is right. British inventor James Dyson spent five years of his life creating 5,127 versions of a product that was not acceptable to the market—the bagless vacuum cleaner.[12] He persevered, and ultimately, struck gold by launching the first such product in the world. He went on to create a multi-billion-dollar company. The Dyson vacuum cleaner is sold in more than sixty-five countries today. Assessing when to persist, and being tenacious, is an important part of being a successful entrepreneur.

Note what happened just a few months after Hike Messenger shut down. During the COVID-19 pandemic, the focus shifted to all things digital, and market conditions were primed for a super-app. There began what *Fortune* describes as the 'gold rush for India's super-app' with conglomerates, retailers, banks, and aggregators pushing to deliver an all-inclusive digital experience to consumers. The scenario became vastly different in 2021-22; sometimes, the market is shaped by extraneous and unpredictable factors.[13]

Borrowing from the country music great Kenny Rogers, we say that in life, as in a game of poker, you have to 'know when to hold them, know when to fold them'. This knack comes with the application of mind and experience.

Key Takeaways

- Failing fast and cheap is contrary to the spirit of entrepreneurship, which requires persistence, resilience and courage.
- Give your idea a fair chance to succeed; successful businesses require funds to scale, and you must have a roadmap to make the cash available.
- Never start a business with the thought of failure, but if it turns out to be unviable, don't continue to pour good money over bad.

5
Early Adopter

PETER DE JAGER

In an earlier chapter, we underlined how vital change is to an organization. In any discussion about organizational change, sooner or later, someone will mention the term 'early adopter'. Immediately everyone will picture a group of people who are willing to be the first to embrace all change. Once the term is raised, the belief is that if we could only identify the early adopters within the organization, we could then enlist them to drive a change forward.

There's just one small problem: the category of 'early adopters' contains as many people as the category of 'unicorns' contains horses with bone spires erupting from their foreheads.

There are no groups of people who are first to routinely embrace any change earlier than the majority of people; there are people who embrace some changes earlier than most. The 'early adopter of all change' is a myth.

In India's twenty-seven-billion-dollar media and entertainment industry,[1] over-the-top (OTT, where content is delivered via an internet connection) holds a market share of 7–9 per cent, which is expected to rise to 22–25 per cent by 2030, while the size of the market held by television is expected to fall from 35 per cent to 24 per cent. An analysis of consumer perception conducted by data intelligence company Axis My India shows that the number of users from tier-two cities is also expected to increase.[2]

Similarly, a study by Deloitte estimated that India would have one billion smartphone users by 2026.[3] In 2021, the country had around 750 million smartphone users. India is also expected to become the second-largest manufacturer of smartphones over the next five years.

Lingraju Sawkar, president of Kyndryl India, a spin-off of IBM's infrastructure services business, has called the Indian market an early adopter of the best and latest technology, and opined that India plays a unique role in bringing technology solutions to the rest of the world.[4]

If 13.5 per cent of the population were early adopters of change (as per the standard bell curve used by Everett M. Rogers and F. Floyd Shoemaker,[5] elaborated later in this chapter), then it would mean that the Indian market is an early adopter of all change. However, this is not the case.

The same study on consumer perception by Axis My India also found that Indians prefer private companies and government-owned companies when it comes to their investment choices—17 per cent preferred the former and 12 per cent the latter, whereas only 1 per cent of the respondents preferred to invest in Initial Public Offerings (IPOs). In spite of an increase in the number of new-age tech firms coming up with them and the growing interest in new-generation IPOs, investment enthusiasts from India are not early adopters of change on this front.

Defining the Category of 'Early Adopters'

Categories are a wonderful human construct. If we can place a thing, or a person, into a category, then we can treat everything and everybody in that category the same way. Why do this? Because it can save us effort and bring some structure to the chaos in front of us. We have taken this idea that 'categories are useful' and applied to how people respond to change. Labelling people as early adopters would be very useful, if it made sense to do so.

We do this constantly for both mundane and complicated situations. When we are doing a jigsaw puzzle, we start by grouping the pieces into a number of different 'sets'—corners, edges and middles—and then we add an additional layer of order, by grouping the pieces according to colours, and then, if possible, by lines and edges, both curved and straight. We do this to make the puzzle easier to solve.

We do similar things with people, grouping them into introverts, extroverts, those that show initiative, those who merely put in their time, those who go the extra mile, those who are reliable, and those who aren't. This list could go on.

The key concept here is that by using categories, we are overlaying a structure on an otherwise chaotic situation, in order to better understand it.

The basic notion of an early adopter is that there are specific individuals, either within our organization or within our target market, who are predisposed to adopting change in general.

Here's how this term is commonly defined and understood by its average user:

> An early adopter is a person who embraces new technology before most other people do. Early adopters tend to buy or try out new hardware items and programmes, and new versions of existing programmes, sooner than most of their peers. According to Everett M. Rogers and F. Floyd Shoemaker, in their 1971 book, *Communication of Innovations*, early adopters make up 13.5 per cent of the population.[6]

If correct, then this is an important category of people for managers to understand better. If we could identify those who fall into this category, what drives them and how better to work with them, then they could be crucial to the success of our change initiatives.

Misunderstanding This Term

Over the past fifty years, our perspectives on organizational change have undergone a dramatic transformation. The consensus once was that change is inevitably chaotic, and difficult, and was mostly resisted at all costs by all parties involved.

That perspective on how we respond to change offered little insight into how to manage change. If anything, it communicated that attempting to manage change is impossible because it is a chaotic process by its very nature, and our best course of action is simply to push change through despite the difficulties, with little consideration to how we might make the transition easier.

Many still believe it is human nature to resist change, and that Machiavelli was wise in his assessment that initiating change was a difficult endeavour. 'Let it be noted that there is no more delicate matter to take in hand, nor more dangerous to conduct, nor more doubtful in its success, than to set up as a leader in the introduction of changes. For he who innovates will have for his enemies all those who are well off under the existing order of things and only the lukewarm supporters in those who might be better off under the new,' he wrote in his political treatise, *The Prince*.[7]

When we make assumptions about what a term means, we end up applying solutions with no relationship to reality. The term early adopter, as commonly understood and defined earlier, is problematic. It describes a category of the general population that simply doesn't exist, it also fails to highlight why early adopters are important to change management strategies. They are opinion leaders.

The common understanding of the term suggests there exists a group of people making up 13.5 per cent of the population who will embrace any change. If we assume this is true, then we will attempt to identify those people before initiating all changes.

Sadly, 'early adopter' has lost all meaning in the field of change management, and is causing more problems than it solves. That's a pity because it, and the terms surrounding it—innovators, early and late majorities, and everyone's favourite, laggards—arose from good research, and when used properly, can aid in our understanding of the change process.

Rogers and Shoemaker, in *Communication of Innovations*, examined the 'adoption levels over time' curves of hundreds of different innovations. They noticed they were mostly the shape of the standard bell curve. Then, for the sake of discussion, they identified different sections of this curve.

The left-most 2.5 per cent of the curve were labelled as 'innovators'. The next 13.5 per cent were tagged as 'early adopters'. On the left of the centre, 34 per cent were the 'early majority', while to the right of the centre, another 34 per cent were the 'late majority'. The final 16 per cent were saddled with the term 'laggards'.

Once Rogers and Shoemaker had these categories, they examined the people occupying them to see if they could identify common denominators beyond their location on the curve. For example, they observed that 'early adopters' were perceived as opinion leaders of the community, with respect to that change/innovation.

It's important to realize these categories had a purely statistical meaning. The early and late majorities make up the core 68 per cent of the curve, as defined by the first standard deviation. The 'early adopters' are the left portion of the second standard deviation. In other words, 'early adopter', as originally intended, is purely a mathematical definition based on the adoption curve for a specific innovation.

It's also critically important and necessary to note that this adoption curve, as defined by Rogers and Shoemaker, only exists after a population has adopted a technology.

And finally, adoption curves do not exist outside the social dynamics surrounding a specific innovation; that is, the same population will generate different adoption curves, if any, for a different change/innovation.

If we lose sight of the following three points, we end up abusing everything that Diffusion Theory can teach us.

1. The statement 'she is an early adopter' is meaningless until associated with a specific change or innovation. For example, I owned a personal computer in 1979, which defines me at the very least as an 'early adopter' of computer technology.

However, I only acquired a cell phone in July 2004, which makes me a laggard of the highest order.

If we understand 'early adopter' to be a personality characteristic with respect to change, as per the first definition, then we are faced with a contradiction. How can I be simultaneously an 'early adopter' and a 'laggard'?

The point is, there is no contradiction here. The flaw is in the general understanding of what 'early adopter' implies. With respect to PCs, I was an early adopter, and with respect to cell phones, I am a laggard. No contradiction exists once we use the terms properly.

Lesson: People do not fall into one change-adoption category; they drift from one to another depending on the specific change/innovation and their personal needs and preferences.

2. The statement '13.5 per cent of the general population is early adopter' is absolutely, totally incorrect.

This statement results in two related and dangerous assumptions:

One, that the complete adoption curve will exist for any change; that is, all change will eventually be embraced by the entire market.

Two, that 13.5 per cent of us will embrace any change.

The evidence that this statement is incorrect is found in two casual observations:

One, at the height of the hula hoop craze, not everyone was hula-hooping.

Two, not even 2.5 per cent of the population has bought a Segway.

Lesson: The adoption terms are accurate only in hindsight; they tell you nothing about how a specific population might respond to a specific change/innovation.

3. 'Early adopter' and the other descriptors Rogers and Shoemaker used to sub-divide the adoption curve are post-facto definitions. They are applicable only after the population in question has embraced a change/innovation. Just because some people take to a change/innovation before others, does not mean that the early and late majority categories are inevitable.

However, what's important in Rogers and Shoemaker's research into the various categories is that the early adopters, more so than the innovators, are likely to be 'opinion leaders'. This suggests the following strategy for using the 'early adopter' category to facilitate a change.

Instead of trying to determine who the 'early adopters' might be before your change, allow them to self-identify their interest. Once they do, find ways to enhance their status as opinion leaders, also known as influencers. Give them a voice within the possible market for your change, either in the general community, your organization, or industry.

The myth of the early adopter is two-fold:

1. That they embrace change regardless of what it might be.
2. That they are important because they embrace your change early, instead of what they bring to your target audience—a passion for what they have embraced and the fact that the early majority looks for guidance.

It would be good to heed what change management consultant Linda Rising says in an article on myths and patterns of organizational change.[8] 'Let the innovators and early adopters lead the way. They can be the trailblazers, the experimenters. Let the late majority and laggards make sure you don't forget the lessons from the past. Never feel that you can discard everything that made your organization great, just because some new ideas are on the horizon. Late majority and laggards are good champion sceptics who make sure you don't just wholesale run over a cliff because you are excited about something new,' Rising writes.

Circling back to India's affinity towards innovations in technology, it's clear what is the driver. An examination of the source of this sudden spurt in the adoption rate of OTT platforms and smartphones will show us that there are reasons why consumers respond to change in the ways that they do.

Sameer Garde, president of Cisco India, credits Mukesh Ambani's foray into the telecommunications market with Reliance Jio for the acceleration of India's digital profile.[9] Data prices fell from Rs 250 per gigabyte in 2014 to Rs 19 per GB in 2018—8 per cent of what consumers used to pay earlier.

The smartphone market is expected to witness a compound annual growth rate (CAGR) of 6 per cent in rural areas, while the urban sector is estimated to grow at a CAGR of 2.5 per cent from 2021 to 2026. This will be largely due to the government's plan to fiberize all villages by 2025 under the BharatNet initiative.

The growing popularity of digital banking services is another example of the influence wielded by external factors on adoption rates. The pandemic and the government's initiatives to push digital banking resulted in a huge increase in transactions through the State Bank of India's online banking platform, YONO. Kyndryl India intends to use the lessons learned from managing SBI's large customer base to design systems for such a huge customer base elsewhere. There are lessons to be learned from why people adopt what they adopt at a certain time and in a certain place.

Companies can leverage this information to create successful models in other contexts.

Key Takeaways

- The concept of 'early adopters' must be viewed in the context of the change they are adopting.
- An 'early adopter' of one new technology may be a laggard for another. Therefore, the concept of early adopters as an inevitable subset of a market doesn't exist.
- Early adopters will accept something new that adds value to their purpose.

Part 2

Busting Myths about Process

6

Best Practices

PETER DE JAGER

The term 'best practices' is undeniably compelling. How can anyone possibly argue against 'best practices'? That's like arguing against the need for clean drinking water; something we have already defined as the 'best'. How can we legitimately find fault with a superlative?

In the early 1990s, one of the up-and-coming best practices was business process reengineering (BPR), promoted by luminaries such as Massachusetts Institute of Technology (MIT) professor Michael Hammer, University of Texas professor Thomas Davenport and James Champy, then president of the CSC Index.[1] The idea was worth considering, though rather simplistic. It advocated that we should take a blank sheet of paper and reconstruct our organization from scratch, obliterating inefficient practices and replacing them with new, more efficient processes, powered by new technologies.

As the latest best practice pushed by consultants and conferences worldwide, it was adopted by many. There were successes, and also many failures.

Following an industry best practice blindly, assuming it's also the best practice for our organization, is inevitably a path toward problems, if not disaster.

In 1995, all three of the primary drivers of this idea—Hammer, Davenport and Champy—issued apologies.[2] In *The Wall Street Journal* (WSJ), Hammer expressed regret that BPR was incorrectly interpreted as a road map to downsize.

We typically use the term best practices when examining our organization and comparing our processes to those of our competitors. We do this for the best of reasons: we want to be certain that we're as competitive, efficient and effective as the rest of our industry. These are noble goals. If every manager, leader and employee made a daily effort to align themselves to these objectives, then our success is almost guaranteed.

This is the lure of the best practices myth. It communicates that industry-wide best practices exist, and if we can identify and copy them lock, stock and barrel into our organization and follow them religiously, we'll succeed.

Part of the problem is that best practice is one of those management terms which is best defined as a buzzword. We've already used the term several times, talked about it and challenged it, yet haven't defined it.

The assumption we're making is that you know what everyone means when we use this term, and that defining it would be superfluous and almost insulting to any reader. The assumption that we all know what the phrase means is part, if not all, of the problem whenever we use buzzwords in our communication. As you read this, you have in your mind either an understanding of what the phrase means or—and this is more likely—you have questions about what it means and you're hoping we define it somewhere in this chapter.

Here's a challenge for you, if you're interested. Ask a handful of your managers, or staff, to one, define a best practice and two, identify the top three best industry practices currently in use by your organization. Then compare these descriptions to each other and focus on where they agree with each other.

If all the responses are in total agreement, then you're head and shoulders above most organizations. The standard result is that the written responses have very little in common, indicating that even if best practices exist within your industry, there is little, if any, agreement on what constitutes an industry best practice. Therefore, there is also little agreement on whether or not you're using a best practice.

Here's one definition of the phrase taken from the internet:

> Best practice means finding—and using—the best ways of working to achieve your business objectives. It involves keeping up to date with the ways that successful businesses operate—in your sector and others—and measuring your ways of working against those used by the market leaders.[3]

This is a compelling definition, because:

1. It suggests a reasonable course of action: Keep your attention on what others are doing.
2. Then it offers advice on what to do with what you discover: Measure your ways against theirs.
3. Finally, it suggests an eventual reward: You too can be a market leader.

As written, this rephrasing of the definition is mostly useful. Knowing what others are doing is a good idea, and measuring our performance against others is equally useful. The last promise is not uncommon when we offer advice—a bit overstated, and often merely motivational.

What's missing in our restatement is the word 'best'. Best by what measure?

I have over thirty years of computer experience. My first computer was an N*Horizon computer; with 64k of RAM, using a Z80a CPU with a processing speed of 4.77khz. Over my career, I owned several dozen home computers and worked for computer companies, service providers, retailers, insurance companies and banks. I have written hundreds of articles for computer magazines and speak regularly at computer conferences to technically skilled audiences.

This is all mentioned, in great boring detail, to establish my technical credentials. I am by all accounts a computer 'geek', a 'nerd', an 'expert' or even a 'maven'. But if you were to ask me for advice on the 'best' computer to buy, you will never get a straight answer. Why? Because my response is always the same. It depends on what you want it to do.

In a nutshell, that is the first of the two problems with the concept of best practices. Best at accomplishing which organizational objective, or objectives? Assume for the moment you're responsible for an assembly line, here are some possible performance measurements:

- Number of finished products per day
- Number of defects per day
- Cost of materials/labour per item
- Amount of waste per day
- Power consumption per day
- Number of workers per shift

- Cost of computer support in total per annum
- Downtime per annum for scheduled and unscheduled maintenance
- Warehousing costs
- Compactness of the assembly line in square metres
- Ability to reshape the line to accommodate design changes
- Maintenance costs per annum

We might also add these measurements to this list:

- Employee happiness while working
- Safety records
- Noise levels during operation
- Levels of employee engagement
- Retention rates
- Labour relations metrics
- Worker demographics

This list is obviously not complete; it is also likely not the list of items you measure in your organization. There might be no other organization in the entire world with the same key performance indicators as the ones your organization considers important. That's the whole point of this discussion. What we value differs from one person to another and from one organization to another.

'Work implies not only that somebody is supposed to do the job, but also accountability, a deadline and, finally, the measurement of results—that is, feedback from results on the work and on the planning process itself,' Peter Drucker wrote in *Management: Tasks, Responsibilities, Practices*.[4] Management is about achieving goals, and those goals are determined by the things we choose to measure.

We could also add 'what we choose to measure determines what and how we manage', or 'until we are clear on what we are measuring, there is no way to determine what a best practice might even look like, or where to search for it'.

We can simplify the issue even further. Consider the project constraint triangle: cost, time and scope. The project manager's 'joke' is to pick any two of these. Our best practice choice depends entirely on which two we choose to value more than the other.

Our organizations differ far too much for there to be a single 'best practice' that applies to more than a handful of organizations. Our organizations are unique for a multitude of reasons; it makes no sense that what works best for the competitor down the street is the ultimate best solution to our unique set of circumstances.

There's another glaring problem with the notion of best practices, and it's made clear in our earlier paraphrasing of the definition: it suggests the eventual reward that 'you too can be a market leader'.

Part of the concept is the notion that if we adopt the practices of the leading companies, then we can be just like them. That's not how one becomes a leader; it's how one becomes a follower.

To be a leader, we must first understand what others are doing, and then go beyond what the current prominent leaders are doing. The advice to go beyond might be the only valuable best practice followed by market leaders. Cartoonist Scott Adams sums it up best in a Dilbert comic strip: 'If everyone else is doing it, best practice is the same thing as mediocre.'[5]

My coauthor Ashok says that any organization's 'practices' should be the right ones. Best practices are those that would be optimum practices for your organization; these are not set in stone and could change from time to time. What is good for your organization at one time need not be so at another. It's equally important to note that what is best for one entity might be entirely inappropriate or awful for another.

What, then, would be best practices? You must begin, of course, by first defining the fundamentals of your organization—the mission, the vision and the values. Practices and processes will follow. Your practices should also be geared toward the state of your company, that is, its growth stage.

Let's take the case of Happiest Health, the media start-up that Ashok launched in 2022. In the pre-launch stage, all the practices across functions were geared toward a single goal: 'how do we progress towards the launch?' During the lead-up, Ashok allowed the team to cut a couple of corners—they were exempt from following routine systems to reach this goal. For example, the team worked without a management information system (MIS)—which has become a vital tool for organizations—for six months. All eyes were only on the launch tracker, with the deadline looming closer.

This was a vastly different scenario from when he started Happiest Minds in 2011. To begin with, it was in a completely different industry, that of information technology. It was a mature industry with set practices and the new company had to follow a defined approach. Ashok also knew where the company was headed, whereas at Happiest Health, Ashok and the start-up team felt their way as they went along. While the company had defined its mission, vision and values, and everybody had to live by those, in its nascent days, the team was still evolving thoughts on content and marketing. It was important, therefore, for the newbie to get these basic strategies in place before starting to crystalize its best practices.

Jacque Vilet, an international human resources expert, echoes this view.[6] 'When reviewing best practices, think about them in terms of whether or not they would be a "best fit" for your company. Best practices need to align with your company's unique needs, culture and business circumstances. The more tailored a practice is for a company, the greater the likelihood of success,' she writes.

'Pursuing "best practice" is a way to stifle innovation,' warns Diane Edwards, a business transformation expert.[7] 'When you look at what others are doing and try to imitate, you will always be playing catch-up. True excellence, surely, must lie in pushing past the existing boundaries. Trying something that no one has done before … and it is innovation and change that will ultimately triumph, long after "best practice" has died.'

Mike Myatt, a leadership adviser to Fortune 500 CEOs and boards, prefers to use the term 'next practices' to get people to focus forward in their thinking.[8]

'Why would you want to do business in the same fashion as your competitors? Don't utilize your competition's practices, but rather innovate around them and improve upon them to create an advantage that can be leveraged in the market. Be disruptive in your approach and don't fall into the trap of doing something in a particular fashion just because others do it that way—think 'next' practices, not best practices. Here's the thing—best practices maintain the status quo, and next practices shatter it, Myatt says.

Amazon is an example of a company tweaking its best practices to suit local markets. In the US and Europe, Amazon's practice is to deliver using well-developed existing logistic infrastructure via trucks, using carriers like FedEx or UPS. China, where Amazon operated from 2004 to 2019, presented an infrastructure challenge, and the company invested in last-mile delivery with its own employees making deliveries on bicycles, according to senior vice-president Diego Piacentini.[9]

In India, Amazon's e-commerce platform began operations in 2013, and the company worked with a host of delivery services. It also set up its own subsidiary company, Amazon Transportation Services Private Limited in 2015 to ship goods from sellers who transact on its online marketplace in India.[10] This helped it to offer services such as same-day delivery and compete with established players like Flipkart in the robust e-commerce market in India.

Manish Sabharwal, vice-chairman at TeamLease Services Limited, a staffing service provider, puts it succinctly. 'Best practices can be a bug and a feature. They can be a bug if they are inflexible, not context-specific, and stifle innovation. They can be a feature if they capture institutional memory; if they create predictability; and if they help handle employee attrition,' he says.

'There are three kinds of knowledge: tacit, codified and embedded. The idea of best practices should be to take knowledge and convert it into codified manuals, etc., and then embed them into the technology and processes of the firm. This means certain areas like operations, customer service, accounting, and logistics with technical problems (rules, players and goals stay the same) are more amenable to best practices than areas like strategy, HR, product development, and corporate finance with wicked problems (rules, players and goals keep changing). So, best practices should be used in areas with technical problems and should be avoided in areas where wicked problems are predominant.'

Organizations can't hold on to a set of uniform practices as the best forever; practices need to be modified, updated or discarded depending on the nature of the business, the stage of life of the business, and that of the market in which it operates.

Key Takeaways

- There are no universal best practices that can be adopted by all organizations.
- Best practices change from time to time, and optimal practices vary at different stages of an organization's life.
- It's better to think of next practices, which will propel us beyond competitors.

7

Automate Everything

PETER DE JAGER

Girish, 24, is a delivery agent, one of the thousands of Indians who entered the delivery market after being laid off during the COVID-19 pandemic. The gig came with its own challenges: increased fuel price led to increasing costs of delivery—it was nearly half a day's earnings. Some of them didn't own a bike and many didn't have a driving licence. What came as a boon to the agents was a micro-mobility vehicle that had been launched as a green solution by Yulu, a mobility start-up based in Bengaluru.[1]

Yulu had set up smart, shared, dockless cycles and electric vehicles to decongest urban areas. The bikes were aimed at public transport users, by bridging first- and last-mile connectivity. Powered by the Internet of Things, both types of bikes could be rented and returned using an app, and payments could be made through a secure digital wallet without physical contact.

Come the pandemic, and there were no commuters to rent or ride the bike.

The bikes, however, came to be in demand from delivery agents, who found that they could slice the cost of delivery, and could save an average of five thousand rupees (approximately sixty-three US dollars) each month. A weekly fee gave them the flexibility of using the bike as much as they wanted, and when the battery ran out, they could simply switch to another bike. Best of all, the battery-operated, lightweight two-wheelers have a top speed of twenty-five kilometres an hour, and don't require a driving licence to ride.[2] Capitalizing on the opportunity, Yulu extended its services to logistics companies, delivery partners and food-delivery aggregators. Apart from offering a green solution to mobility, the electric bike enabled cheaper delivery costs, which meant cheaper delivery rates for customers.

The example above is a splendid one of successful automation—the technology works, it's simple and it brings about a direct and positive impact on lives and the community. There's absolutely no question that automation has changed life rapidly and radically.

Both the authors of this book have a decades-long vested interest in the use of technology; we've both made our living using computer technologies to bring value to our clients. Deploying technology and automating processes is a large part of our success. So, it might seem more than just a little bit strange to include 'automate everything' as a problematic myth or suggestion in any way in this collection. It's almost like we wish to kill the goose that lays the golden egg.

All computer programmes contain 'bugs' of some sort. A joke in the computer industry is that the only bug-free programme is the one we've deleted. In many ways, the observation that all programmes contain flaws—some hidden, some all too apparent—is trivial. Even so, it often raises objections from those who might naively insist their software is bug-free. Be wary of these people; they know not whereof they speak.

More troublesome is that the flawed nature of software is all too often ignored. This can, has, and will forever, cause problems ranging from the mundane (when your word processor insists your spelling of a word is incorrect, when you know it isn't) to the catastrophic (when a Boeing 737 Max aircraft crashes, resulting in the death of hundreds, due to unexpected problems with onboard automated computer systems).[3]

If every computer programme has bugs, then it follows naturally that the more complicated and complex a system becomes, the number of bugs it contains will increase in a non-linear fashion as the problems interact with each other, creating new, and totally unexpected outcomes.

If you need any evidence that the use of computers involves significant risks, then The Risks Digest forum, operated by the Association of Computing Machinery (ACM) and moderated by Peter G. Neumann, is the primary source of computer error reporting since it was launched in 1985. The forum is populated with reports and discussions of all types of computing and technological failures and the resulting consequences. The reports are filed by both information technology practitioners and academics worldwide.

If we rely on computers—and in the twenty-first century we all depend on them—then it's well worth our investment to browse the 'risks' list from time to time. At the very least, it'll keep our minds open to the risks involved in handing over too much control to computers.

While the above observations are true and even obvious, they're not the primary reason why 'automate everything' is problematic.

Even though all computing is flawed, we can mitigate those risks and reap the obvious benefits offered by technology. It would be ludicrous to suggest that we should avoid all these risks by simply not automating anything. For starters, it would be hypocritical to write this essay on a computer, taking advantage of at least several dozen, if not hundreds, of different computer applications to do so, and then call for the abolishment of computing. The issue with automating everything is more subtle than the issues described, and more problematic.

Assume for the moment that it is possible to write perfect applications, ones that never make mistakes. They do exactly what we tell them to, with no ambiguity, no mistakes and no mismatch between the specifications and the final product. In this impossible-to-achieve fairy tale world, the advice to automate everything is still bad advice, for two distinctly different reasons.

First Scenario: Automating Chaos

Early in my career, I worked as an internal IT consultant for a retail holding company. One of the divisions had a chain of about 180 stores situated across Canada. This was in the late-1980s, when PCs were just beginning to enter the business world.

Senior management had bought into the productivity promise of what PCs could do for the organization. They wanted to automate everything and started a project to place a PC in every store across Canada. I was placed in charge of the project and allocated the budget necessary to get the job done. For a computer technology professional, this was a dream project. The mandate was simply automate everything in the stores.

Their reasoning was that store processes were chaotic, and they would rely on the productivity power of PCs to bring order to that situation. How exactly we would accomplish that was never discussed. The solution was assumed even before the problem was defined. Their solution, the outcome they wished the computer department to deliver, was a PC in every store from coast to coast.

Technology doesn't fix a chaotic process. That's not how technology works. It cannot automatically bring order out of chaos, any more than the hammer and saw in your workshop can build a house, a boat or even a lowly toothpick.

Technology is a tool, devoid of functionality until used by someone who knows what they want it to do, and has the skills and the resources—time, money, knowledge, determination and perseverance—to do it. Ultimately bringing their vision of the final product to life.

People tend to see 'technology' as the answer, even before they know what the question is. This perspective of a supremely capable technology is endemic, and has several variations.

The directive 'automate the payroll system' assumes that we know what we want the system to do. Payroll requirements are vast and varied. What is best for a company distributing tiffin lunches in Mumbai won't even scratch the surface of payroll system requirements of a multinational telecom company based in New York City. Likewise, that payroll system used very effectively by the company in NYC would fail miserably if used by the tiffin lunch company in Mumbai.

Technology doesn't offer off-the-rack solutions; we must tailor it to meet unique and specific needs.

Once again, this observation is obvious, but if you're a computer person, you're asked, 'what's the best X' and told to 'automate Y' constantly without any hint of the final objective. There's a difference between what organizations say they understand, and the questions they ask that display the flaws in their understanding. Sometimes their response, when challenged, is, 'we know what we want it to do. We want to use technology to automate what we're currently doing'.

Technology isn't just a tool, it's a particular type of tool. Technology is the ultimate lever, it amplifies our current situation regardless of what it is. If our organization is chaotic, automation will make it more so, and it will ensure that the chaos is faster, deeper and more efficient. It will not solve the root cause of the problem of why our organization is in chaos. If our organization is efficient, automation will make it more so, and we should automate everything sooner rather than later.

This brings us to the second scenario—while the sentence I just typed above sounds perfectly reasonable, it is also deeply flawed. There are good reasons not to automate efficient processes.

Second Scenario: Automating the Efficient

In a subsequent chapter, where we discuss the myth 'if it ain't broke, don't fix it', we mention the music industry of the 1980s and 1990s. The same example is useful here.

Assume that you were placed in charge of an automation project for a music company. From the recording studio to the manufacturing process, where Nusrat Fateh Ali Khan's voice is stamped on vinyl, packaged, sent to warehouses, and then to distribution centres, placed on trucks and sent to stores, placed into inventory, sold, and the sales analysed to determine what is and isn't selling.

Opportunities for automation exist at every stage of this process. The potential cost savings, if done correctly, are significant.

There's a reason I'm using such a well-known example. It's obvious today that automating every stage of the process is the wrong approach, because we know that the entire chain of activities was made obsolete by a totally different approach to the problem made possible by new technologies.

Once upon a time, the easiest way for you to pay me some amount of money was to write a cheque. I would then take that slip of paper to my local bank branch and they would cash it and either hand me money, or deposit the amount into my bank account. The use of cheques as a way of moving money from one person or company to another is vanishing from society. It's been replaced with technology that removes the need for a paper slip, and any physical interaction with a bank. Several digital applications allow us to transfer money: Interac, PayPal, Venmo, GPay, Paytm, PhonePe, BHIM UPI, Mobikwik, and PayUMoney, to name only a few of the dozens available globally.

Technology is a tool, and while we can reap benefits from it to automate our tasks, the instant we believe that the users of the technology don't have to understand how it works, we run into problems.

An industry specialist in business process automation solutions, ThinkAutomation, wisely cautions that automation is a complex process.[4] 'Automation software is capable of complex processes. It can run workflows with several steps and data touchpoints, using advanced layers of "if" rules. And it does so accurately and efficiently,' the firm states. 'But sometimes during complex processes, you need human intervention and decision-making. If it's a process that demands significant human attention at many stages, don't try to automate it all. Instead, automate the smaller, simpler segments. This is about using automation as a tool to help your human employees increase accuracy and efficiency in completing their most complex tasks. Just don't attempt to automate the entire process.'

Another major worry that comes with automation is job loss. This apprehension is not without backing. The editors of this book, for example, rely on apps that provide automated transcriptions and grammar checks, which has made an entire layer of workers redundant. (P.S. The final output is vetted by human eyes too.)

It is useful to note that the automation that came with the Industrial Revolution did not hinder employment and wages, since the new technologies maintained the role of the human being in value creation. However, with AI, the array of tasks where human beings have a competitive advantage is reduced. The handful of companies that dominate AI technology view removing fallible humans from the equation as an imperative. Governments are also subsidizing these organizations through tax breaks and interest deductions. The result is that adopting automation technologies has become profitable, even when the technology in itself is not productive. Focusing solely on automating further and further without thinking about the reasons for automation is leading to low productivity and a lack of innovation.[5]

Both Ashok and I are technologists; we're strong believers in the notion that despite the inherent flaws in all systems, they can—when we understand their limitations and increase our understanding of their potential—deliver transformational change within our organizations. Part of that understanding is to never automate chaos, or even efficient processes, if the available technology can provide very different, more effective approaches to delivering the desired outcome.

Key Takeaways

- Never automate a chaotic process. Fix the process first.
- It's not advisable to always automate the entire process. Automating the smaller segments in the process might yield better results.
- Never automate today what will be obsolete tomorrow.

8

If It Ain't Broke, Don't Fix It

PETER DE JAGER

Captain James Cook was one of the great explorers of the eighteenth century. Among his many accomplishments, he was the first European to discover the eastern coast of Australia, and the first known person to circumnavigate New Zealand, apart from being instrumental in mapping Newfoundland off the east coast of Canada.

There's no denying Cook was a great navigator—he mapped the world armed with only a traditional sextant, and John Harrison's breakthrough timekeeping device, K1, the first instrument to provide a precise measurement of longitude. He solved the problem of navigation through the solutions available in his time.

But what if we could step back in time and hand Captain Cook a working GPS? (We'll ignore what it takes to get a GPS working and keep it working—a sky filled with two to three dozen satellites, electricity and an understanding of Einstein's

Theory of Relativity, among others) With the ability to measure exactly where he was at all times, how much more could he have done in his already impressive lifetime? With no disrespect to John Harrison's K1 chronograph, it was a cumbersome, complicated contraption compared to the GPS hidden away in the smartphone in your pocket.

But we can't go back in time. Such 'what if' musings are science fiction, and while they might be interesting, such an intervention in world history is beyond our ability.

Well, not exactly.

While we can't assist good old Captain Cook, we can do something similar for our organizations. But only if we throw away the bad advice 'if it ain't broke, don't fix it'.

Think back to our organizations of twenty or even just ten years ago. It is no speculation on our part to state that at that time our organizations, faced a variety of problems, which we solved with technologies of the time, just as Captain Cook seized upon the K1 as the best available solution to his longitude problem. If the GPS had been available, he'd have chosen that instead, but it wasn't. He made do with what he had at hand.

That's what organizations always do; we make do with the solutions of our time, but times change, and so do the solutions available to us.

We live in a busy world, where we have neither the time, nor the budget, to do all the things we could do, and possibly should be doing. Therefore, the advice if it ain't broke, don't fix it is, at first glance, good advice. It supports ideas such as 'stay focused on your goals', and related time management strategies, such as adhering to the central idea within the Pareto principle—focus our resources on just those activities that generate the best outcomes.

In its own way, it's almost redundant advice. When we're busy, our attention is kidnapped by the latest crisis, the upcoming deadline, and the deluge of daily distractions. To use another old saying, 'the squeaky wheels get the grease', and solved problems fade into the background noise of the day, and they don't clamour constantly for our attention. We don't need to be told to leave them alone; we honestly don't even think of them.

The suggestion that 'if it ain't broke, don't fix it' is a good strategy becomes problematic when someone raises the possibility of reexamining an existing business process, in light of newer, more effective solutions. Rather than listening to their revelation of how we might do better, we brush it off by repeating, without considering their idea, 'if it ain't broke, don't fix it!' It's how we typically defend the current status quo from the never-ending threat of change.

Like many of the 'myths' we're exploring, it contains a germ of truth and only becomes an issue when we apply it constantly, using it instead of thinking about the situation we find ourselves in at the time.

It's also closely related to other one-line management 'strategies' that we use to avoid the possibility of change, such as 'we tried that before and it didn't work', or our personal favourite, 'we've always done it that way!'

The origin of this advice to avoid reexamining old solutions is lost in time, but the most likely candidate for making it popular is Thomas Bertram Lance, director of the Office of Management and Budget in Jimmy Carter's 1977 US administration. He was quoted in the US Chamber of Commerce's 'Nation's Business' newsletter in May 1977 (p. 27)—the rest of his quote was, 'that's the trouble with government, fixing things that aren't broken and not fixing things that are'.

Our organizations are filled with old fixes that could be replaced with solutions made possible by newer technologies. This happens far more often than we realize.

Here's one of the most visible examples: the music industry once had a solution to its need to distribute music; it built brick-and-mortar stores all over the world. (Yes, both the authors are that old.) This was a successful multi-billion-dollar business with a monopolistic lock on how consumers accessed music. The internet arrived at about the same time that compact discs (CDs) became available to the consumer. The music industry moved away from analogue recordings on vinyl records and towards digital music. The instant it did, the world of music distribution changed.

The internet works by sharing files that are digital. Once the music industry made its music digital, it was able to distribute music to the desk of the consumer via the phone line. This solution was implemented in 1999 in the form of Napster, a peer-to-peer music-sharing network, but not by the music industry. Napster was implemented originally by the consumer. This new solution to the already solved problem of music distribution via brick-and-mortar stores is a classic example of reexamining a solution already in place and coming up with a totally new solution only made possible by a better approach.

The challenge we face is the old stumbling block, 'if it ain't broke, don't fix it'. Our old solutions work. We're not compelled to upgrade the solutions we implemented way back. Record stores worked, and they continued to work until the new solution became dominant, and now they don't. When was the last time you went to a music store to buy music?

So, the question we should constantly ask is, what old solutions exist in our organizations that are crying out for reexamination, in light of new abilities? This is a difficult question because solutions that are working are almost invisible, even to those looking for them. We only notice problems, the things that grab our attention by constantly annoying us. Those things that were solved a long time ago fade into the background.

There are many examples of businesses that failed because they didn't fix their 'business'.[1] Kodak, Xerox and Blackberry lead an illustrious list of companies that stayed so focused on doing things the way they always had that they failed to lead innovation, let alone anticipate what was coming. And when the inevitable changes driven by technology rocked their markets, these companies found themselves floundering in the same markets that they once led.

Orkut, the social networking service owned and operated by Google, could have been the world leader in social media—it was number one in countries like India and Brazil. But the company didn't focus on this business, and instead, ceded the space to Facebook.

The downfall of India's star automobile brand, Hindustan Motors, is a notable example of failure due to complacency.[2] In 1958, Hindustan Motors began manufacturing the wildly popular Ambassador cars. The car was a status symbol, a marker of success and wealth, and an embodiment of bureaucratic power.

However, the company that produced the king of Indian roads lost its market footing in the 1980s.

Prior to that decade, the Indian automobile industry, like most other industries, was heavily protected by the government through restrictions on competition and foreign investment. The intention was to create a level playing field for Indian companies. Hindustan Motors was satisfied with the patronage it was receiving and found no reason to innovate. Few technical innovations were made over two decades, with most of the improvements having only an aesthetic quality.

When the market began to open up in 1991, Hindustan Motors found itself facing competition from multiple other car manufacturers.

The Indian middle class now had a number of options, one of which was the Maruti 800, a car that would go on to take the Indian roads by storm. By the end of the 1980s, Maruti Suzuki held the biggest share of the market. When new manufacturers arrived at the doorsteps of Indian customers, Hindustan Motors failed to advertise and leverage its brand name to boost sales, and did not offer any technical upgrades. Outdated production techniques meant that cost was high and output too low. The quality of after-sales service was also outmatched by the new players.

There are lots of other simpler examples; some are almost trivial, and others would require a rethinking of how we design our cities, how we manage our people, and even how we shape our organizations.

Bright Lights

The advances in light-emitting diode (LED) technology are, in a word, astounding. While not appropriate for all lighting needs, we are grossly negligent if we're not examining all our lighting needs and determining where moving from old lighting solutions to the latest technologies makes financial and environmental sense.

If we needed a financial reason to fix this one thing in our organization that's working perfectly, then consider just two data points.

- Energy savings when moving from incandescent to LED lighting is in excess of 80 per cent.
- Incandescent lighting has a mean time between failure (MTBF) on the high end of 20,000 hours, and LED lights have an MTBF on the high end of 100,000 hours, greatly reducing maintenance costs at all levels.

These are just general figures—obviously, your details will depend greatly on the application, but the ratios are heavily in favour of LEDs.

Social Media

If an organization includes a communication component of any sort in its activities, and especially if it doesn't, there are at least a half-dozen or so new technologies and even new behaviours in play within our communities that are worth examining.

How exactly could the current state of social media affect your organization? Figuring it out is the point of this exercise. New abilities provide advanced, and sometimes hidden, opportunities, as well as their own unique problems. Until we reexamine what we've done in the past, we have no idea what we might do in the future.

Communications

Here's the bottom line on communications. Twenty years ago, even ten years ago, there were a limited number of communication channels available: TV, radio, mail, telex, fax, print media, billboards, knocking on doors and communicating from a soapbox on the street corner. Perhaps a few others. Today? Nearly everyone carries all of that and much, much more in their pocket all the time. How have we capitalized upon this immediate and compelling new media channel? Most of us haven't, because what we're currently doing is, 'it's working, don't break it!'

An outstanding example of social media success is Barack Obama winning the 2008 US presidential elections.[3] A study by Stanford University outlines how this little-known senator ran against household name and former First Lady Hillary Clinton for the right to represent the Democrats in the presidential election, and went on to become the first African–American to be the President of the United States.

'Obama won by a margin of nearly 200 electoral votes and 8.5 million popular votes. Many factors contributed to his success, but a major one was the way Obama and his Chicago-based campaign team used social media and technology as an integral part of their campaign strategy, not only to raise money, but also, more importantly, to develop a groundswell of empowered volunteers who felt that they could make a difference,' the Stanford study notes.

Going to Work

Let's circle back to the concept of office and work. Why do we insist that people go to the office? In the past, that's where the work was. An accountant needed to go to the office because that's where the books were. Today, we can access those books from anywhere in the world. We don't have to physically relocate ourselves each day, clogging up the roads and polluting the air. We merely have to log in to the system to do what we need to do.

Slow changes had begun with telecommuting becoming acceptable, and it was on the rise. There were obstacles of course.

The primary one is that 'this isn't how we've done it in the past'. Management's primary objection is that people must be physically close to us, in order for us to properly manage them. But along came COVID-19, and the worldwide pandemic led to lockdowns. All of a sudden, in the blink of an eye, work-from-home (WFH) became the norm. Why? Because we were forced into a different way of working. Necessity is the mother of invention.

Even with COVID-19 turning from a pandemic into an endemic situation, management is having to deal with employees demanding that they be allowed to 'WFA' (work from anywhere). Increasingly, it looks like work could be a hybrid model of employees coming into the office a few days a week and working from home or a cafe or the beach. As long as they have internet/data connectivity, they can log in to work and video conferencing, and stay connected and productive.

New technologies offer us the opportunity to reopen old problems. Sometimes, doing nothing more than asking 'what if X had been available twenty years ago?' prompts us to zero in on those opportunities hidden behind old solutions.

An important exercise that Ashok suggests that you do would be to visualize situations where someone thinks that something is broken and wants to set about making a change. Especially when they come into an organization from outside, and particularly so, if the organization is not doing well, the tendency is to think that everything is wrong. They would want to begin to change and overhaul everything. What would be a better course of action is to prioritize the areas which they see are broken, and then only work on those. If they look at the whole organization as a mess, it would compound the problem.

Take, for instance, when Ashok moved from a fan manufacturing company to a refrigeration business (as you will read in detail in the chapter 'People Resist Change'). The new company had made losses for five years and reached a negative net worth, but he turned it around with the same team. He only fired one person, but realized that the team was fine. His advice? 'It would be very good to examine what's broken, before trying to fix it.'

The other angle is to ask yourself this: the company might not be broken today, but is it likely to be broken? Ashok advises that you should stress-test it, and if you anticipate that it could happen, you should start making the change before it breaks.

Key Takeaways

- With change and innovation constantly evolving, the myth of 'if it ain't broke, don't fix it' would lead to disaster.
- Test the process and move pre-emptively to avoid it breaking.
- It would be very good to examine what's broken, before trying to fix it.

9

PowerPoint-Type Presentations Are Boring

PETER DE JAGER

Quick question: would you rather read this article, or have it screened for you as a PowerPoint presentation? If you got to this chapter in the book, we already know the answer!

No one would fault you if, after attending a presentation of any sort—be it a conference keynote, a sales pitch, a project update, a budget meeting or a monthly management meeting—you are bored to the point of feeling tortured. Whether it is PowerPoint, Prezi, Inpres, Rocketium, Google Slides or any other presentation tool, chances are that viewing tiny black, barely legible rows of text staggering across a white screen in a darkened room, as the presenter drones monotonously, lull us to sleep.

'Death by PowerPoint' is a perception that's influential enough to prompt decisions like the ones made at Amazon, where Jeff Bezos banned PowerPoint in presentations,[1] and Harvard University's claim that PowerPoint negatively affects both information transfer, and the brand of the organization using it in presentations.[2]

Before we make this decision to abandon modern presentation tools, consider the images found in the Lascaux Caves in France. About 20,000 years ago, one or possibly more of our ancestors crawled into the depths of a dark, damp cave, lit a flickering flame, and with some charcoal and coloured pigments, painted depictions of human activities and surrounding wildlife. Far from being boring, these are awe-inspiring expressions of artistic genius.[3]

We like old sayings that have stood the test of time, and here's one relevant to this discussion: 'a bad workman blames his tools'. There's nothing fundamentally wrong with any of the presentation tools available to the modern cave painter, aka the corporate presenter. However, there is something definitely and undeniably wrong with how we use these tools.

After we read a poorly written book, or article, we never blame Microsoft Word, or whichever word processor was used to create the book. We place the blame where it belongs: on the writer. It makes no more sense to blame the presentation tool used to create a boring talk than it does to blame the word processor, or the pen and ink used for a bad book.

An important part of the problem is how we've chosen to label these tools by calling them 'presentation' tools. Therefore, we perceive them as the means by which we will 'present' something to an audience. We slap the information onto a slide, usually, in bullet points, display it on the screen, and then say something about the data.

In order to totally squash the myth that 'PowerPoint is boring' we must first step back a bit, and ask a preliminary question. How should we use presentation tools to present information?

This is a trick question, in that it isn't a single question, but two important ones clubbed together. 'How should we use presentation tools,' is the obvious one. The less obvious one is how to present information.

How Should We Use Presentation Tools?

We must first accept that when we present information/data, we must engage the attention of the audience. Unless the audience is listening, no information transfer takes place. So, let's start with the basic problem: how do we gain, and hold, their attention for the length of a budget meeting, project update, or expansion plan?[4]

When we present, we enter into a competition for the attention of those sitting in the room. The competitors for their attention might or might not be in the room. They include cell phones, work deadlines, stray thoughts, in-room distractions, the state of current politics, the smell of doughnuts and coffee, and whatever else is going on in their lives.

In an ideal world, everyone in the room is hanging on our every word. We don't live in that ideal world; we live in a busy one. The problem is that we don't have much if any, direct control over any of the myriad distractions vying for their thoughts. Telling people to turn off their phones helps a little bit, but honestly, not much. Authority demands compliance; it doesn't guarantee attention. Telling them to pay attention has the opposite effect if they are older than five, though I suspect it never worked at that age either.

To move towards a solution, we need to understand exactly how PowerPoint (or any similar tool) works. By that, we don't mean the syntax of using the tool, but instead rather how we respond to what it can put on the screen. For the moment, we're going to ignore all use of images, transitions, animation, colour and graphics, and focus on the simplest of PPT usage; that is, black words on a boring white background. I offer three observations:

First, when we put up sentences on the screen as the presenter, we tend to read them aloud. If you need evidence of this (always a good idea), observe yourself during your next few meetings—which slides do you tend to read out to the attendees word for word? Most likely, it's the ones with full sentences, not the ones with terse bullet points.

Second, we should never read from the screen. Why? Because once we place something on the screen, the audience has already read it. When we then take time to read it aloud to them, they are immediately bored. They already know what we're going to say, and their ever-wandering mind is thinking about whether they'll be ordering red or white wine at dinner tonight. Therefore, our objective is to gain their attention, and never let go of it.

Third, people seek meaning. We all need to make sense of the world. We can exploit this strength/weakness to seize the attention of anyone watching our presentation.

Compare the following two mini-slides:

Biodata of Peter

Born	:	January 1955
Place of Birth	:	Durban, South Africa
Marital Status	:	Married

and

Biodata of Peter

Date of Birth	:	__________
Place of Birth	:	__________
Marital Status	:	__________

When we see the first slide, everything is communicated to us. We no longer need the presenter, and we immediately seek something else to pay attention to—red or white wine tonight?

The second slide is significantly different. It tells us what information to expect. It doesn't present us with that information; it prepares us to receive it if we're interested. To receive it, we must pay attention to the speaker. We're not presented with any other options. Our attention is no longer optional, it's required.

In theatre or writing, this is known as 'foreshadowing'. It's used to create tension, mystery or suspense, to draw the audience into the story, and to connect the thoughts of the meeting attendee to what's going on. It engages them.

The mistake commonly made with any presentation tool is to forget that the speaker is the central point of focus, and to place everything on the screen. Here's another example:

Top Three Project Risks

- Delivery of Module X (on schedule)
- Testing Handoff (three months behind schedule)
- Import License Approval (six-month delay expected)

and

Top Three Project Risks

-
-
-

Once again, the first slide tells you everything you might want to know, and now you go back to texting your spouse. The second slide tells you I'm going to talk about three risks, and now, you need to pay attention. The assumption here is that project risks are relevant to those in the room.

One entices you to listen, and the other forces you to read and leaves nothing for the speaker. Obviously, there's much more than could be said about using PowerPoint to engage an audience, but this is the key concept. If we wish to hold their attention, we must use what we place on the screen to focus their attention on what we want to say, at the speed we want to say it, in the sequence we need to say it. This leads us to the second question.

How Should We Present Information?

Why speak? Why get a crowd of people into a room, and speak to them? If the goal is only to distribute information quickly, clearly and precisely, then sharing a hardcopy report or a link to an online post is vastly more effective.

The goal, and the strength, of speaking to a room of people is in its ability to communicate a message. When you read this sentence, we, the authors, Ashok and Peter, have no idea if we're communicating with you. We can't see your reaction. Are you nodding your head in agreement? Or rolling your eyes?

That isn't true when we're speaking to you around a conference table, watching your reactions to our words—a presenter knows if they're getting through to the people in the room as they are speaking. That has huge value if the objective is to communicate.

We finally get to the flaw in most presentations: despite the ability and potential of a presentation to communicate a message, there is no clear message. A question worth asking of every presentation we give is, at the end of the ten or thirty or sixty minutes of presenting, what do we want the listener to take away?

If your reason for making a presentation is not crystal-clear in your head, we humbly suggest you don't present anything. You'll waste your time and that of your audience. You'll also do lasting harm to your reputation and career. (By the way, when speaking, blatant repetition is not only allowed, it's a recognized tactic to ensure that the audience takes away what you want them to take away.)[5]

We fail to deliver in two ways:

1. We attempt to deliver far too much information in the time available. A simple guideline is to have one key message

for every thirty minutes of the presentation. This does not mean that only one bit of content is communicated every half hour; it means that everything in a half-hour relates to a single message.

2. Many presenters are incapable of answering the question, 'what's the key message you're trying to communicate?' They lack focus. There's no goalpost they're working towards. They're 'just talking', and chances are, the audience is 'just sleeping'.

Here are some simple guidelines[6] for crafting and delivering the takeaway message:

- Engage the audience from the start—ask a pointed question related to the takeaway message.
- If what you want to say doesn't relate to your message, jettison it. Stay focused.
- Throw away the fancy words, keep the language simple. Don't hide the message behind ten-dollar words.
- Tell stories to illustrate your message—this is how we connect.[7]
- If you want to talk about risk, talk about any common practice where we take precautions.
- If you want to talk about trust, talk about a small child at the edge of a pool, and its mom saying 'jump!' as she holds out her hands.
- Closing statements should crystalize the message.

All of the above assumes something important: when we stand up in a meeting, we do indeed have a message to communicate. That's indeed the opportunity we have in front of us, each time we're presenting to others. The success of a presentation is more than 99 per cent due to the speaker, and less than 1 per cent due to the tool they're using.

Ashok, the coauthor of this book, has a different take on the use of PowerPoint, which he believes has limited utility. He says one should never begin a meeting with a customer with a PPT. If you are going to talk to a customer sitting across the table, you don't need to make a presentation. If you are in a room with them and you get up and make a presentation, odds are that the customer will be bored. What the customer really wants is a dialogue. You can always do a presentation in the second or third meeting, when technical details need to be discussed.

If someone needs to make a presentation to him, Ashok asks that the deck be sent to him at least forty-eight hours prior to the meeting. Going through the presentation before a meeting saves time and energy; he might have a question to ask about something mentioned in slide one, the answer to which is going to be in slide five. Having gone through the presentation in advance, he might just cut to the chase and focus on a certain section.

When David Yoffie joined the board of MindTree, he and other board members sat through a PPT on the company's strategy. Yoffie, who was on Intel's board for twenty-nine years, told Ashok that Intel had done away with strategy presentations and had opted for narrative notes instead. Ashok agreed with this as he had been using summaries from the beginning of his career—there were no computers or PPTs then!

Though it is almost impossible for people to stop using presentations, Ashok has been trying to minimize them. And when they are absolutely essential, he feels that presentations should never be longer than five slides.

Frank Hedler, director of advanced analytics at Simpson Carpen, notes in his article for ResearchLive that PowerPoint is completely outdated.[8]

'What marketers and insight professionals really need today is the ability to easily consume data on-demand ... And they need to be able to share these insights with others in the business via intuitive interfaces, without the need to create a deck of PowerPoint charts,' Hedler writes.

Key Takeaways

- Presenting/communicating/engaging is a human activity; don't blame the medium for a poor presentation.
- Keep your presentations focused and relevant.
- Use the appropriate tool for different settings: PPT, narrative notes and intuitive interfaces.

10

Multitasking Is to Be Always Avoided

ASHOK SOOTA

The attempt to be more efficient and productive through multitasking has been getting a bad rap over the last few years. Multitasking has been blamed for inducing absent-mindedness and reducing creativity.[1] Researchers from the University of London[2] and the University of Sussex[3] have also found that multitasking leads to reduced IQ. The latter group found that individuals who spent more time using multiple devices simultaneously had less brain density in the anterior cingulate cortex. This is the part of the brain that is responsible for emotional and cognitive controls.

There is an equally illustrious line of scholars and researchers on the other side of the argument. Scientists have found an upside to multitasking, and say that it boosts creativity. By activating your brain and widening its cognitive flexibility, multitasking paves the way for more creativity—an important finding, especially since contemporary life is defined by fast-paced workplaces and a multiplicity of things to be tracked.

Many people engage in multitasking, both in their professional and personal lives. Some tasks are simply done on autopilot. Sipping morning coffee while reading the newspaper. Eating dinner off a tray while watching TV. Walking in a park or on the treadmill while speaking on the phone. Writing an email when talking on the phone, or checking messages on smartphones while attending meetings.

People multitask in the hope of getting more things done in a shorter period of time. It has become so insidious that they are hardly able to spot it when they are doing it.

Our view is that while there are many instances where multitasking is counterproductive and even objectionable, when done correctly and at the appropriate time, multitasking can contribute to improving productivity. How and when you can multitask varies between the three worlds that we inhabit: physical, virtual and personal.

Physical World

Multitasking should not be done in a public environment or in a physical meeting, where it could be perceived as inattention or rude behaviour, and may also distract the speakers. Here are three examples where multitasking was inappropriate.

In November 2013, India was playing the second cricket test match against West Indies at the Wankhede Stadium in Mumbai. It was Sachin Tendulkar's last-ever international match, and fans in India, and perhaps the cricket-playing world, were following with great interest. So was the case at the national council meeting of a large industry association, where a galaxy of CEOs were glued to their tablets and mobile phones. So much so that when Tendulkar was out for seventy-four runs, the president of the association announced that perhaps the assembled CEOs would now focus on the meeting. This is an example of multitasking at the top level.

The second example is an annual meeting that I chaired as the outgoing president of another industry association. The CEO of a multinational company, who later went on to become an entrepreneur, never stopped going through his emails during the meeting. We were sitting at a circular table, and I could clearly see what he was doing. This is an example of bad manners.

The third example is more recent. I attended an event where speakers were distracted by a person in the front row. He appeared to be looking at his mobile for most of the event. He could have been tweeting about the event, and perhaps, amplifying the brand message. But to the onlookers, it seemed as if he was multitasking without following what the speakers were saying. Such a lack of social manners could have discouraged the speakers. This is another instance of when someone should not multitask.

In the real world, appearances are important; not only should you focus, but you should also appear to be focused. It is true that it isn't easy to focus on two or more tasks at the same time. Looking at your phone while attending a meeting will, without doubt, reduce the attention you devote to the speaker. Multitasking of this sort is impolite and rude. Worse yet, you might not absorb the unspoken dialogue or body language that could have helped you. These instances are not necessarily the best use of time and energy, or even application of the mind. I don't allow people to have bilateral conversations in a group meeting. This is certainly not the place to multitask, and I call out people who do so. When a meeting is in progress, everyone must focus on it; otherwise, we would be getting into many meetings because of the lack of focus by some.

Virtual World

The scenario changes dramatically in the virtual world. You can easily focus on the meeting even while multitasking. Here, you are able to do so without as many problems as in the real world. Virtual conferences and webinars that you get invited to may take up half a day or a whole day. My personal way is to line up what you want and need to do, which will not distract the meeting. Put yourself on mute so you don't trouble other people, and then you get on to multitasking. You can still pay attention to what's going on, as long as you stay alert. You can choose to intervene whenever you want to do so, or are required to do so.

Why I believe multitasking isn't always a bad thing can be attributed to our experience of doing virtual road shows during the COVID-19 pandemic. As I have mentioned in the second edition of my book *Entrepreneurship Simplified*,[4] six of us in the leadership team collectively saved 42,000 person-hours as each of us was required to speak for only ten minutes at each session. In contrast, the physical roadshows used to stretch over seventy-five minutes. I presented the opening and the last slides, and answered questions at the end. The time that I was not required to speak or be seen, I used for my yoga practice, which I would have missed during the morning and afternoon roadshows. This is an example where multitasking is certainly an efficient way of using your time.

Juggling Act

I think a CEO in particular is a person who can juggle multiple worlds. This doesn't mean that you sit in a meeting and do multiple things. What it means is that you have to skillfully and efficiently juggle multiple balls. Some of the most successful people seem to be able to navigate more than a few roles, and very well at that.

Elon Musk, when he's not posting on Twitter, is the CEO and chief engineer of SpaceX; CEO and product architect of Tesla; founder of The Boring Company; and co-founder of Neuralink and OpenAI. He even finds time to make appearances in films and television shows. He's not an exception; there are several people we know who do many things quite well, simultaneously.

Each person handles their time differently, between their work, interests and passion. We asked Nandan Nilekani how he handles his various roles, such as the non-executive chairman of Infosys, and the multiple other organizations and non-profits that he has set up or supports. He does take up monumentally huge national tasks, such as setting up the Unique Identification Authority of India (Aadhaar) and the Open Network for Digital Commerce (ONDC).

'If the definition of multitasking is switching from one task to another every couple of minutes, I don't multitask. I work on multiple big ideas, but it's not multitasking. I'm actually very focused. If I'm doing a meeting at Infosys, I blank out everything else and focus only on Infosys issues. If I'm doing a meeting at ONDC, I'll focus only on that,' Nilekani told us in conversations for this book. 'I keep my life very simple. I don't have WhatsApp. I use my laptop for work. My mental mode when I'm on my iPad is browsing; it's for curation. My phone is for communication.'

Nilekani eschews social media, and anyone who wants to communicate with him can call, send a text message or email him. He practices a zero-inbox strategy. 'I clear all my emails first thing in the morning, last thing at night, and perhaps in between. I finish that day's tasks there and then. When I go to sleep, I sleep like a newborn baby. The next morning is a fresh day,' he outlined.

He also has no interest in trivial pursuits on social media even, if the rest of the world has joined the bandwagon: he would rather use his free time to do nothing. It all boils down to priorities; he has written an entire book about not having too many distractions, titled *The Art of Bitfulness*.[5]

I agree with Nilekani that when you focus on a given thing, you have to focus completely. You can compartmentalize your time and set periods for when you shift from one task to the other. For example, I tried different methods before finding one I think is the most effective in dealing with the multiple entities that need my attention, and not get distracted by parallel matters. Early in the morning, I spend twenty minutes each on emails regarding Happiest Minds, Happiest Health, SKAN and the family office. I deal with emails concerning each organization one by one. I'm able to finish responding to all my emails. That's 100 per cent focus for twenty minutes for each organization in turn, and as a result, I never get distracted. However, that doesn't prevent me from multitasking in between.

Multitaskers are often accused of suffering from attention deficit hyperactivity disorder (ADHD). Multitasking and ADHD are certainly not the same. A person who is in a meeting and apparently focused may have a mind wandering all over the place. On the other hand, a skilled multitasker may be able to handle two (or more) tasks concurrently with complete concentration, and do justice to both.

A simulated study conducted by Shimul Melwani, organizational behaviour professor at UNC Kenan-Flagler Business School, and Chaitali Kapadia, assistant professor at Florida International University, found that multitasking did not have any impact on the participants' analytical performance;

rather, it did result in an outflow of a significantly higher number of ideas.[6]

But what continued to confound them is why multitasking boosted creativity, but negatively affected many other vital functions of the brain such as attention, concentration and listening. Further inquiry showed them that there is a direct link between brain activation and increased creativity. By making more demands on our attention, multitasking induces our brains to activate more resources to meet the demands. The spillover energy results in cognitive flexibility, and consequently, more creative outputs.

An implication of the study is that it shows us how we can manipulate creativity by organizing our work in certain ways.[7] Surely, a data-heavy or detail-oriented assignment is bound to suffer if we employ multitasking. At the same time, if the task at hand calls for an outflow of creative ideas, then it might make sense to energize and boost your brain by dabbling in more than one task simultaneously. I have found that I do my best thinking while I'm swimming. This is a creative and positive way of engaging in multitasking.

Prioritization

Given the fact that human energy is finite, common sense dictates that if there are a number of tasks to be accomplished, one would be able to accomplish more in less time if some of those tasks could be combined or dealt with simultaneously.

There are different ways of being efficient. One school of thought says that when you have multiple tasks to accomplish, it would help to make a checklist of tasks, in order of priority, and then tackle them one by one rather than attempt to do them all together. This does not mean that you don't move on to the next task until you have completed the previous one. For example, you have initiated an email enquiry, or sent a message. While you wait for the reply, you don't have to sit idle. You can move on down the list.

It is very clear to me when you can multitask, and that is when you are idle. I carry this to somewhat absurd lengths at times. I can't bear to stay idle during the lag time before my computer boots up, and I will always have something handy to work on or look at. If there's a paper that I want to read, I want the paper next to me just on the chance that I have the time to read it. You must experiment and choose what works for you.

In your personal world, watching the news while you are on a treadmill, listening to a podcast as you drive or cooking as you video-call friends or family are good ways of multitasking.

Key Takeaways

- Never multitask in physical meetings, where it would be seen as rude or disengaged from the programme.
- The virtual world presents an enormous opportunity to improve your efficiency and productivity by multitasking. You must ensure that you are effectively engaged with all your multitasking activities.
- In your personal world, the skill of handling multiple tasks can be put to good creative use.

Part 3

Busting Myths about People and Organizations

11

We Are Under-Led and Over-Managed/ Over-Led and Under-Managed

PETER DE JAGER

We tried to find the originator of the myth 'we are under-led and over-managed', and all we could find were tons of articles and blogs propagating the same idea, with no one claiming to be the oracle who first made this statement. The conclusion we drew is that the statement gained strength through gurus who, in order to emphasize the importance of leadership, chose to denigrate management. This is quite a familiar pattern in management books/writings. For example, if an author wants to emphasize execution and implementation, they will go overboard and make it sound like the only thing that's needed for business success is execution.

The stream of articles on this myth has created a backlash, leading to the opposite myth: we are over-led and under-managed. One example of a guru who propounds this is Jim Collins.

Both groups choose definitions that suit them, leading to non-sequitur reasoning that leadership is more important than management or vice-versa. But to quote G.K. Chesterton, philosopher and writer, 'all generalizations are untrue, including this one'.

We will describe later why both these camps are misled, but first, let's examine the reasoning each of them use to propagate their arguments and line of thinking.

Under-Led and Over-Managed

Let's start with the under-led and over-managed group, and 'leaders have a tendency to praise success and drive people, whereas managers work to find fault'.[1]

There's 'a game-changing difference between managing and leading,' says Jeremiah Sinks.[2] 'Businesses are managed but people are led. A great leader gets the willing participation of others to follow a vision,' he explains.

Here's another from Brigette Hyacinth. 'Leaders command respect. Managers demand it.'[3]

Or take this: 'A good leader puts the interest of their followers before their own and measures success by whether their follower is better off.' We want to ask, 'and managers don't'?

Yet another quote: 'Leaders recognize that everyone is motivated differently. Managers, on the other hand, believe people will be motivated if you pay them enough. Leaders understand that pay is a satisfier but not the only motivator.'

If you define leadership in this glorified way and negate management, you can definitely claim that leadership is greater, or better, or more important than management.

Perhaps the most encompassing and most misleading or erroneous is the following table:

Managers have subordinates	Leaders have followers
Managers use an authoritarian style	Leaders have a motivational style
Managers tell what to do	Leaders show what to do
Managers have good ideas	Leaders implement good ideas
Managers react to change	Leaders create change
Managers try to be heroes	Leaders make heroes of everyone around them
Managers exercise power over people	Leaders develop power with people

Most of the above are convenient definitions to further the argument that leadership is greater than management. One point is completely erroneous. Most literature says that leaders have great ideas, while managers implement them. The point we find most amusing is that 'managers have subordinates' while 'leaders have followers'. The concept of leaders and followers is great for social media, but in an organizational context, it's best to think of teams where persons can be leaders/managers or team members, and can rotate these roles as the need arises. Also, having followers reminds us of the Pied Piper of Hamelin.

Finally, we quote Warren Bennis, who has given us many management truths, but with whom we disagree on this one: 'Failing organizations are usually over-managed and under-led.'

Later, we will give you a few examples that give a different perspective.

Over-Led and Under-Managed

Let's now come to the over-led and under-managed school of thought. The leading arguments for this come from Henry Mintzberg, in his book *Simply Managing: What Managers Do — and Can Do Better*.[4] 'It has become popular to talk about us being over-managed and under-led. I believe we are now over-led and under-managed … Some leaders now believe their job is about coming up with big ideas. They dismiss executing these ideas, engaging in conversation and planning the details as management work,' he writes.

'Corporate America has had too much of fancy leadership, disconnected from plain old management. We're over-led and under-managed. As someone who teaches, writes and advises about management, I hear stories about this every day: about CEOs who don't manage so much as deem, pronouncing performance targets, for instance, that are supposed to be met by whoever is doing the real managing,' Mintzberg goes on to say.[5]

The plus point of Mintzberg's arguments is that he is not bashing leadership (in the way the other camp bashes management), but is bemoaning the styles of leadership that he believes have become superficial, and which avoid getting into depth.

Randy Mayeux, a professional speaker and writer, has also weighed in on the debate.[6] 'I think Mintzberg is both right and wrong. He is right—we are under-managed. But he is wrong—we are not over-led. Too many organizations are, sadly, both under-managed and under-led,' Mayeux says.

We are not as pessimistic. We even see the glass as more than half full. Many, many organizations are correctly led and correctly managed, though everyone can keep improving continuously. At the same time, one cannot deny the truth in Mayeux's statement that some are under-led and under-managed.

Another argument from the 'over-led and under-managed' group is that good execution beats good strategy. Our counter is that you need both good leadership and good management to succeed, and the argument of what or who beats the other is inconsequential.

This now brings us to our belief—to be successful, a professional must be a good leader and a good manager—and we believe that both are equally important. Likewise, for an organization to succeed over a period of time, it must have good leadership and good management.

Leadership and management are two sides of the same coin, and complement each other. Leadership is about shared vision, providing a sense of purpose, motivation, organization building, succession planning, empowering and mentoring.

Management is about planning, measuring and executing. It is also about the basic discipline and rhythms of running a company; about processes and systems and functional expertise.

Both leadership and management have a key role in risk-taking. All business is about taking risks; leaders must take risks, but it is their managerial team that assesses the degree of risk, keeping it from spinning out of control. So, while a shared vision is essential for aligning the organization and giving a sense of purpose, it is management that executes it to make it a reality.

Leadership and management are not mutually exclusive. Professionals must exhibit both traits throughout their careers. Accordingly, we find it strange when Ross Ashcroft expresses that 'tragically, some of the best managers have been rewarded with leadership positions'.[7] Every job—from a level where you become responsible for a team—has both leadership and management content.

It is fair to debate how much time a professional should spend on leadership versus managing. However, we would not be overly prescriptive, or define any ratios, as many authors do. This will vary from time to time for different roles, and will even depend on organizational structure.

For example, consider a chief executive who reports in one instance to an executive chairman, and in the other, to the board through a non-executive chairman. In the first instance, the CEO will support the framing of a vision, which the executive chairman will have the primary responsibility to articulate and create. Both of them have the responsibility of propagating the vision to make it a shared vision across the organization.

When the CEO reports to a non-executive chairman, the role shifts dramatically. It is now the CEO's prime responsibility to articulate the vision. The same would apply to the formulation of strategy and decisions on mergers and acquisitions, where the role of the CEO changes towards more time needed for leadership.

Failures and Successes

Think about some of the most glaring failures in business, as well as some of the most amazingly successful ones. The lesson is that the failures suffered from both bad leadership and bad management, while the successful ones flourished due to great leadership and great management.

Let's consider Enron and Kingfisher Airlines as examples of failures. Both had high-profile, indeed glamorous, leaders at the helm, and for a while, made huge waves of apparent success. Both collapsed suddenly and swiftly. A common factor in both was poor leadership, as manifested by poor corporate governance. Poor management for Enron was reflected in their accounting practices.[8] In Kingfisher's case, founder Vijay Mallya was so obsessed with his grand vision of creating India's best airlines that he let the company's cash position dwindle to the extent it could not keep all its aircraft flying. The sudden cancellation of many flights precipitated the downward spiral and demise of the company.[9]

Examples of sustained success for us are GE (in Jack Welch's time), Microsoft, and Google. Jack Welch had a great vision of being in the top two or top three worldwide in every business sector. The processes, systems and management he instituted were also legendary. When one business in GE decided to institute an 'order to billing to collection' process, it got executed in every business.

Microsoft had a driving vision of a computer on every desk and, later, to be the leader in software for the office. Its continued success over forty years is a testimony to its strong leadership and management, though it may have faltered during the Steve Ballmer years.[10]

The other success we would like to recognize is Google. The founders, Larry Page and Sergey Brin, could see that mobile search would overtake desktop search, and hence, they gave Android an important place in their vision. The best testimony to Google's strong management is that it is the only company in the world that continued to succeed and flourish when Microsoft entered into its prime business.

'A collision of opposites is the answer to over-managed or over-led. Find some leaders who scare you. Hire some managers who drive you crazy. Over-managed organizations need disruptors. Over-led organizations need system builders,' suggests Dan Rockwell, a leadership coach and consultant.[11]

We concur with Manish Sabharwal, vice-chairman at TeamLease Services Limited, a staffing service provider, who told us, 'management, leadership and entrepreneurship is a continuum, and neither is more important than the other'.

Sabharwal said it's all about balance. 'My favourite quote comes from politics: "you campaign in poetry but govern in prose". When I was younger, I thought there was a poetry phase, which was followed by a prose phase. But now I recognize it is about balance: too much poetry and no prose, and you get nothing done; too much prose and no poetry, and you do nothing great,' he said.

This leads to our conclusion that good leadership and good management are both necessary for sustained success. It is not necessary to make an artificial distinction on which is more important.

Key Takeaways

- It is a myth that organizations are over-led and under-managed/under-led and over-managed.
- Leadership and management are not mutually exclusive; they are two sides of the same coin. At times, leaders must manage and managers must lead.
- People thrive in an environment of balanced leadership and management.

12

We Can Train People to Become Leaders

PETER DE JAGER

Here's an exercise for you, dear reader, that might shed some light on why we believe that teaching people to become leaders is more than a little bit optimistic. Create a list of at least a half-dozen, preferably more, individuals whom you consider to be leaders. While I suspect that many of you will gravitate towards 'political' leaders for several reasons, try to include an equal number of leaders from other walks of life—business, personal or religious.

The primary reason for taking the time to list these individuals is that your personal view of what makes a leader is far more important, relevant and useful to you, than any dictionary definition. (The rest of this chapter will have less meaning for you if you've chosen not to make this list.)

It would also be useful to you if you took the time, after creating this list, to put in writing your personal, 'formal' definition of leader. You could go one step further; you could, if you choose, score the people on your list by this definition.

On a scale of 1–10, how does each person on your list match your formal definition? Are there any noticeable anomalies? Is there someone who ranks low based on your definition, but is still on your list? Why? Where does the discrepancy arise?

(Naturally, this approach works better in a discussion, either one-on-one or in a workshop. But for the moment, all we have is this medium.)

When I've had the opportunity to do this in a workshop, here is a consolidation (in no particular order) of the most frequent mentions:

Dalai Lama
Edward Snowden
Nelson Mandela
Chesley
Sullenberger
Steven Harper
Jesus Christ

Donald Trump
Barack Obama
Richard Feynman
Steve Jobs
Henry Ford
Bono
Sakichi Toyoda

Justin Trudeau Bill
Arrowsmith
Mahatma Gandhi
Margaret Thatcher
Abraham Lincoln
Winston Churchill
Walt Disney

Based on this list, it's obvious that who we consider a leader is a personal choice. I'm sure that some of these names are unknown to you (I had to look up some of them). Others, you might believe, have no place on any leader list for various reasons. You might decide there are still others who, upon reflection, are 'better' than some of those on your list. Some you might consider more 'hero' than 'leader'; others you might exclude for other reasons. It's worth noting that to some people, these are their leaders regardless of what someone else might think.

(A lesson here is that who we choose as leader differs from person to person—there's not a single definition of a leader that works for everyone.)

The reason for the two lists, your own and the list above, is to attempt to give examples of what we usually mean when we think about leaders—a far more effective approach than reading a collection of definitions. That said, we can return to this notion that we can train people to be leaders.

Think of a handful of people in your organization whom you do not currently consider to be leaders. It doesn't matter if they are managers or not; the only requirement is that they are not, to your mind, leaders. This is the third list we shall refer to later.

Now, do you believe that any of the people on your third list could be 'trained' to be the equal of, or even come close to, any of the leaders in your own list, or the list I've offered?

To clarify your resources for this 'leadership training' project, let's say that you can send any of the 'non-leaders' you identified in your organization to any leadership training course offered in the world for a year, and you have a training budget of one million US dollars.

Could we, with all the resources we could muster, create someone worthy of the first two lists?

If not, then why not? What is it that's common to all the individuals on the first two lists, that we cannot instill in someone who doesn't have it, regardless of how much training we provide?

Based on my experience with this question, there are several responses to this thought experiment.

The first is that the people we list as leaders are extraordinary individuals are driven by circumstances, passion and ultimately, a decision to take a personal initiative in some manner to achieve a personal desire or objective.

We can manipulate circumstances to some extent, placing people in situations where the only way to succeed is to take up the challenge and act. Good managers can use delegation to place possible leadership candidates into situations where initiative is necessary to succeed, and then step back and hope that a leader emerges.

We can create environments where passion is rewarded, and the reward tailored to the individual we're trying to launch into a leadership role. Sometimes they will decide for themselves that there is a goal worth striving for far more than they have in the past.

But what we cannot do is instill in them whatever it is that creates the fire in the belly—the thing that compels someone to act on their own, to personally decide that they must assume a leadership position. We can lead people up to the edge, but getting them to take the leap on their own is not something that can be taught.

The next objection to this notion, that we cannot train people to be leaders, is a fair one—the people on both lists are extraordinary. That's a result of how you were asked to create your leadership list: you only list the most extraordinary examples of leadership that come to mind, and of course, it's impossible to take an average, less-than-average or even slightly above-average person in terms of ability and turn them into that type of leader. It's an unreasonable objective.

To dial back the difficulty of the goal of training someone to become a leader, let's ignore the list of extraordinary leaders, and present a different objective.

Return to your handful of non-leaders—the third list—you were asked to consider earlier. You chose to add individuals to that list, using whatever internal definition of leader that resides in your head. For each individual on that list, ask the following question: are they not leaders because of a lack of opportunity, or because they've simply displayed no interest in leading others?

Now, the question becomes simpler: do you think any amount of training can turn someone, who doesn't have a desire to lead, into a leader? If someone has never shown initiative, coached someone, 'taken' the lead when a group of people is having trouble deciding how to solve a problem, or picked up the marker to summarize points made in a meeting, can they be taught to be a leader?

On the other hand, is there anyone who has shown initiative, has naturally taken the lead in a meeting, has seen someone having difficulty and then assisted them without being asked to do so, has constantly offered ideas during a meeting, or has put in the extra effort to get something done? They are already leaders. Nascent ones perhaps, but leaders nevertheless.

It's obvious that many people not only believe it's possible to train people to become leaders, but that this type of training is effective at producing leaders. A significant amount of money is spent on leadership training—global spending on leadership training is in the range of 350–400 billion US dollars.[1] The corporate leadership training market is expected to grow by 15.78 billion dollars between 2021 and 2025. India is one of the countries where the market for leadership training is expected to expand during this time.[2]

Despite the belief that we can train people to become talented leaders, and the number of resources thrown at doing exactly that, there is widespread global agreement that finding talent to fill high-level positions is, to put it mildly, difficult.

A January 2020 study from www.manpowergroup.com reported that 54 per cent of companies globally reported talent shortages. For example, 69 per cent of companies in the USA, 47 per cent in Italy and 41 per cent in Spain reported significant difficulties in filling key senior-level positions. Are corporations 'victims of the great training robbery', as Michael Beer, Cahners-Rabb professor of business administration, emeritus, at Harvard Business School, says?[3]

Somewhere, there is a disconnect between what the leadership training industry claims to be able to produce, and the global shortage of people required to fill senior positions in our organizations. One might be tempted to suggest that this notion that we can train people to become leaders is wishful thinking—one we're willing to invest huge amounts of money in, despite our seeming inability to produce enough leaders to fill critical positions.

Part of the problem might be the lack of cohesiveness in how we define certain terms. For starters, there's the eternal discussion on how 'leaders' differ from 'managers'. I divide the two terms as follows:

Managers maintain the current course of an organization/department efficiently and effectively, maximizing results using available resources.

Leaders have all the responsibilities of managers, combined with the task of setting and implementing a new course for the organization/department.

To put it another way, managers maintain the status quo (which might include implementing a change initiative handed to them by a leader), while leaders initiate movement toward a new and improved status quo.

Defining a leader is even more contentious. Dictionary definitions are of little help here, as they tend to be somewhat 'circular' in how the term is defined. Of these, I gravitate more towards the definitions offered by Vocabulary.com: leaders almost inevitably require followers; without them, the concept of leadership loses all meaning. Commanding someone to do something, part of Webster's definition, isn't 'leading' them. Having influence over others is closer to the common understanding of what leaders bring to the table.

Rishikesha Krishnan, professor of strategy and director of IIM-Bangalore, pointed out to us that there has been a lot of debate about the difference between a manager and a leader. 'It can be said quite safely that we are fairly good at producing managers. Leadership is a little more difficult to impart in an MBA programme, though there are leadership courses, including a popular one that takes students through literary classics, examining leadership styles portrayed in books over the years,' Krishnan said.

What then, you might ask, is the relevance of business schools? The challenge in consistently developing and training leaders, Krishnan said, lies in the fact that 'to a degree, leadership cannot be learned in the classroom … You need to put people in actual work situations. You need to give them challenges; you have to be in the frying pan to develop those leadership abilities,' he stressed.

IIM-B applies the 'crucible of leadership' advocated by Warren Bennis, a pioneer of contemporary leadership studies, in the executive education programmes that it conducts for companies. In one instance, during an extensive leadership development engagement with a company, the institute crafted realistic crucible-type situations and roles, which would enable people with leadership abilities to sharpen those with coaching, mentoring, etc.

Revathy Ashok, a distinguished alum of IIM-B and co-founder of Strategy Garage, also heads B.PAC, an initiative that encourages civic leadership. To the question of whether leaders can be trained, she answered, 'this is a tough one'.

'I think the answer is a "yes" and a "no". Sometimes the raw material is exceptional, and you can carve the most beautiful sculpture with the right tools to sculpt it. Sometimes the raw material is not very good, but as you keep chipping away, it sort of starts becoming better and better,' she said.

Organizations, she explained, can play a big role in building the leadership pipeline, giving training, exposure and tools. The level of absorption may be different for different people.

Having worked closely with countless executives in various companies, my coauthor Ashok Soota's view on this subject is that a person must have an innate ability to grow into a leader, and training will act as an add-on and supplement. You can support a person with training by giving them an executive coach, but these would only work for people whom you have already spotted as having leadership ability, by helping them bridge the gap, if any.[4] The coaching and training support would not be of any use if they lack natural talent, and they would go through training without benefiting from it. On the flip side, he's seen many successful leaders who never got a coach or training; he's among such people who did not get such inputs at any point, and grew in the course of the job.

The leadership training industry cannot teach anyone how to become a leader for the simple reason that nobody can teach someone else to take the initiative—that attribute comes from within. The industry can teach someone who is already a leader how to become a better leader by introducing teachable skills: communications, people skills, time management, organizational skills and problem-solving. Even creativity and innovation are teachable, but not the inner spark, the fire in the belly that compels someone to take action when others choose not to.

Are we then saying that an organization does not need to invest in leadership training? Certainly not, the industry has come a long way beyond where training can be shelved. The question is not whether an organization benefits from leadership training. The question is, what happens after leadership training? What happens after the chosen few come back from their all-expenses-paid course?

Michael Beer and his coauthors note in the article cited earlier that 'only one in four senior managers report that training was critical to business outcomes'. It would be pertinent to note their conclusion that leadership training should be part of the organization's 'capability development strategy', which includes clear metrics for review.

Here's a twist in the tale. Victor Lipman, management expert, author and speaker, posits an interesting theory that upturns the conventional view of leadership traits.[5] In his book *The Type B Manager* Lipman says that while people with Type A personalities are considered to have leadership qualities, the qualities that drive them to success—such as being competitive—would not motivate employees. What you need as a manager is a Type B person, with a calm and low-key personality, who will foster relationships, navigate conflict and earn trust.

In recent years, leadership training for high-potential executives has included, apart from classroom courses and outbound programmes, workshops in yoga, vipassana, and such, to help tap into various other dimensions of leadership. And perhaps, create a blend of personalities!

Key Takeaways

- People can be trained to become leaders only if they have innate leadership capabilities.
- Leadership training is more difficult to impart than management training.
- Leadership skills are better developed on the job as a practitioner.

13

Empowerment Is about the Authority to Make Decisions

PETER DE JAGER

The following scenario might be playing out even as you read this—you're collaborating with a half-dozen people on a large project that is expected to last about a year; it's a complicated endeavour, there are a lot of moving parts, and each of the individuals involved has different sets of skills and areas of expertise. And most importantly, the project is significantly larger than what one person can handle on their own.

This scenario isn't that unusual; you're likely active in such a group. Now add two more elements to this common configuration:

1. You're the manager of this group. At this point, there's still nothing unusual about this hypothetical project. It's almost a working definition of a project team.

2. Everyone needs your permission to do anything related to the project. The sound you just heard? It's your project coming to a screeching halt, or at least shifting to a lower gear, where it will creep like a glacier towards that future deadline.

As managers, we know that having to ask for 'permission to act' slows down any process. Of course, for a few managers, this is exactly what they are comfortable with. When we demand that people ask for our permission to act, then we control everything, thereby giving us power over others. This management style has a name—micromanaging. Those of us who have suffered under such a manager know exactly why it's problematic. When we're being micromanaged, we feel that our competence isn't trusted.

There's another reason for this level of micromanagement, besides the desire to maintain control. We refer to this situation as the 'expert's dilemma'. This is where a manager believes that they, and only they, have the necessary expertise to make the 'best' decisions, and are reluctant to allow anyone else to make less-than-perfect decisions. This is slightly different to the controlling manager example, because it's not based on a desire to control, but a desire to always apply the best solution possible, and believing that only the manager knows what's best.

The 'solution' to demanding that people 'ask for permission' is to embrace a totally different way of managing. We choose to allow people to make their own decisions, without having to ask the manager for permission to act. This management philosophy is called employee empowerment, and is defined most commonly along these lines:

> Employee empowerment is an approach to management that recognizes that processes are impeded by the need

> to request permission for every action, or input to every decision; it thereby promotes a culture of full autonomy for all employees, within well-defined limits, to make independent decisions and act on them.
>
> Empowerment is a management approach on the far end of a management style spectrum, with micromanagement on the other end.

The myth here is that if we decide to give our people the authority to make decisions, we've created a culture of empowerment, and we've done our job.

For the moment, we'll ignore the myth hidden here, accept the definition at face value, and explore how a manager moves from the initial need to micromanage to the realization that empowerment is the answer they didn't know they were seeking.

Our first task as new managers is to put aside some of our misconceptions about management. We're not assisted in this difficult task by the very title we're assigned. The word manager seems to imply at least some, if not full, control over what our people will be doing. Why? Because we're their manager, we're supposed to manage them; one of the dictionary definitions of manage is to control.

The first rude awakening we have is that people have a mind of their own, and will inevitably do what they believe they should do, and not necessarily what we want them to do.

So, to make sure that what we need to be done is done, we might choose to do it ourselves. We micromanage, both by hovering over people's shoulders as they attempt to do what we've asked, or we simply don't assign tasks—we do them ourselves—because 'if you want something done correctly, then…' We'll leave it to the reader to fill in the blank.

Eventually, sooner or later, the penny drops, and we accept that if we are to succeed in our new role, we must learn to leverage the efforts and expertise of our team to get a multiplier of our own output which, in our new station in life, are the people who report to us. How long does it take for this proverbial penny to drop? It varies. We know managers who haven't learned the lesson in twenty years; on the other end of the people skills spectrum, some naturals delegate on their first day.

I was a slow learner, as I have admitted. It took me three long and painful years before I realized that I would be more effective as a manager if I could bring myself to rely on the six extremely capable people working for me. To do that, I needed to first decide that I could give up daily control in exchange for long-term productivity increases. That was the difficult part, becoming willing to give up control. The easy part was learning how to delegate.

Managers who delegate well leverage the potential of their entire team to new heights. We know the existing skillsets of our people: their individual points of brilliance, and the areas that could improve with practice, coaching and guidance. Assigned tasks either leverage the existing brilliance, or are used as training to perfect weaker skillsets. Delegation done well isn't just about getting work done, it's an integral part of succession planning. Delegation is a form of education and an invitation to long-term growth. Delegation, done properly, will also create an excellent team and shape the careers of those who work with us.[1]

However, if we really want to supercharge our organizations, there's an additional step we can take; the one we started to discuss earlier. We can decide to 'empower our team'. We can give them permission to make their own decisions, which is to uncouple 'action' from the 'need to get permission' to act.

Requesting permission to do anything takes time, which could be put to better use, like doing the thing.

Most readers nodded their heads in agreement as they read the earlier definition of empowerment, but something crucial is missing. Something critical with respect to 'empowerment initiatives'.

An issue that's often raised is the issue of 'scope'.[2] It's all very well to empower people, but that doesn't mean they can make any decision they want. An operations manager can't decide on their own to break ground on a new town hall, or open a new market in a foreign country, or merge with a competitor. None of those is their decision to make!

This is obviously true, and highlights the necessity to define the scope of empowerment. Defining the scope of control for each team member isn't an easy task, but it's worth doing. While most scopes are almost obvious, we must define the boundaries of 'empowerment'. Each person should know what types of decisions they can make, otherwise, empowerment won't end well.

While 'scope' is important, and the initial definition barely mentioned it, it's still not the missing critical component of empowerment.

This highlights the glaring flaw in the original definition. Empowerment isn't about 'the permission to make decisions'. It's about 'the permission to make mistakes, without fear of undue consequences'. This also includes the permission to experiment, which will inevitably lead to a few failures.

While empowering the team, the manager must reserve the right to receive information, but resist the temptation to barge in and intervene at the drop of a hat. How many times have we witnessed the creation of task forces and teams to analyse mistakes/failures, even while the team is working out solutions? All empowerment must have boundaries.

This is obviously connected to the issue of 'scope'. People should not make decisions, even when empowered, that are distinctly outside of the domain of responsibility. The reason is that if they make poor decisions outside their scope, those mistakes are unacceptable—and the recognition is that they are far more likely to make poor decisions outside their scope of responsibility and expertise.

The test of your empowerment culture will inevitably arise when a well-intentioned team member makes a poor decision within their well-defined scope of responsibility. What happens then, if the consequences of making a poor decision are perceived as too harsh? Then the 'empowerment culture' you are attempting to instill in your organization will fail. Your capable team members will immediately stop making their own decisions, because the downside risk is too high. The key to empowerment, therefore, is to give them the right to make mistakes without undue consequences. This right must be accompanied by course correction.

The benefits of empowerment go well beyond the person who empowers and the team which is the beneficiary of the empowerment. This leads to the creation of an agile organization. Effective empowerment is aligned with the vision and objectives of the company, a key prerequisite of creating an agile organization.

To quote McKinsey & Co, 'agile organizations are characterized as a network of teams operating in rapid learning and decision-making cycles'.[3]

Furthermore, when team members feel empowered, they also feel trusted. Motivation levels improve and they have a higher feeling of ownership and belonging. When customer-facing persons are empowered to solve a customer problem (including making financial commitments within limits), it also increases customer satisfaction and organizational credibility.

Given the importance of empowerment, it's worthwhile here to understand the barriers which come in the way of effective empowerment (though these are not pertinent to our theme of myths to be demolished). For this, we feel the best approach is to quote from a blog post by Agile Vietnam.[4]

From the aspect of the organization:

- Lack of trust between manager and staff.
- No clear definition and policy of accountability.
- Empowered staff do not receive enough training to be able to handle the empowerment.
- No differentiation between staff.
- Lack of communication.
- Unclear vision.

From the aspect of the manager:

- Unwillingness to give up control.
- Reluctance to change management style.
- Fear of losing position.
- Clinging to old accountability.

From the aspect of staff:

- Do not want to be accountable.
- Do not realize their value and potential.
- Fear of losing position due to new accountability.
- Lack of training.

Since empowerment is a powerful and useful concept, one of the requirements is that all team members share the same vision of the future organization. All decisions must be made with the idea that the decision will advance the organization towards a common goal.[5]

Without this coherency of vision, we're faced with a situation where highly capable people might be making decisions that are dragging the organization towards several, non-overlapping destinations. That opens up a totally different set of challenges. The scope we define for empowerment should have an objective in mind. Otherwise, we speed up the organization's move towards chaos.[6]

Susan Heathfield, HR and management consultant, offers a holistic view of empowerment. 'People think that someone, usually the manager, has to bestow empowerment on the people who report to them. Consequently, the reporting staff members wait for the bestowing of empowerment, and the manager asks why people won't act in empowered ways. This bestowing and waiting has led to general unhappiness, mostly undeserved, with the concept of empowerment in many organizations,' she says.

Instead, one should think of empowerment as the process of an individual enabling themselves to take action, and control work and decision-making in autonomous ways, Heathfield explains. 'Empowerment comes from the individual. The organization has the responsibility to create a work environment which helps foster the ability and desire of employees to act in empowered ways.'[7]

Gustavo Razzetti, marketing and innovation consultant and founder of Fearless Culture, says we should forget empowerment, and encourage autonomy instead. 'Stop trying to empower your employees; people resent being controlled. Try autonomy instead. Create a culture of trust: establish clear rules, hire the right people, and let them do their jobs,' he recommends.[8]

Ashok, the coauthor of this book, is of the view that time management is all about empowerment, which would then create discretionary time for the leader. Most often, when people talk about time management, they are referring to improving productivity. There's no better way of improving productivity than empowering others to do the job. Once you have done that, you release tonnes of discretionary time that you can use for more strategic work.

Ashok doesn't believe in quarterly reviews, though all those who report directly to him submit their quarterly reports. His reasoning is that if he sits down with them for a review, he ought to be adding value to them. If they are proficient in their job, and he has read their quarterly reports and knows how their work in the company is progressing, he prefers to empower them to continue to do their job without taking up their time for a review. He chooses instead to sit down for reviews with new hires.

The process he follows is for them to begin by sending a weekly report, then fortnightly, then monthly, until they don't need to sit down with him anymore.

He has also collapsed the layers of reviews by choosing to combine the reviews he would carry out in his dual role as CEO and chairman. The quarterly reviews come through the board increasingly, instead of him doing it as the CEO. Instead of taking up the time of the top executives twice over, he prefers to do it at one shot, at the board level, as the chairman. This empowers the team to get on with their jobs while freeing up discretionary time for themselves. This does come with the possibility of some critical comments coming out at the board meeting, but there would also be some positives and praise.

A study by Allan Lee, Sara Willis, and Amy Wei Tian offers interesting and rather surprising insights.[9] To summarize:

- Empowering leadership does not lead to uniform results. It works best in motivating certain types of performance and certain types of employees.
- Empowering leaders are much more effective at influencing employee creativity and citizenship behaviour (that is, behaviour that is not formally recognized or rewarded, such as helping coworkers or attending work functions that aren't mandatory) than routine task performance.
- Empowering leaders are also more likely to be trusted by their subordinates.
- Empowering leaders were more effective at influencing employee performance in Eastern, compared to Western, cultures. Their study found that empowering leadership was not always welcome in Western cultures, and employees viewed the extensive care and concern shown by an empowering leader as an intrusion or even an attempt at informal control.
- Empowering leaders had a more positive impact on employees who had less experience working in their organizations.

Key Takeaways

- Empowerment should include the permission to make mistakes; otherwise, people will shy away from taking risks.
- Organizations must create an environment that encourages an individual's desire for empowerment.
- Empowerment benefits the leader, the team and its members, and the organization by increasing productivity.

14

People Resist Change

PETER DE JAGER

When I was about fifteen years old, my family packed up what little we had, left South Africa, and emigrated to Canada. This type of change, a transition from an initial 'state' to a different 'state', is life-altering. Organizations deal with change too, and often encounter resistance from the people within them. Later in this chapter, you will read about how two exemplary leaders—T.T. Jagannathan and my coauthor Ashok—dealt with resistance to change in their organizations.

The world changes daily. If there is one fact we can bet on, in addition to death and taxes, it is that yesterday is not today, and today will bear little resemblance to tomorrow. As to more distant horizons, we best be prepared to look to our children for guidance as we become strangers in a strange land.

In this maelstrom of change, there rests this core belief that 'people resist change'. This belief is the reason why there are shelves of business books and truckloads of university courses on change, and more workshops than we could ever have the time to attend. All intended to answer the key question: 'how do we overcome resistance to our corporate changes?' To put it another way, most of these books, courses and workshops exist only because we believe that 'people resist change', and that change is somehow a problem for organizations. If not, we would buy no books, attend no courses nor sit on hard seats in long workshops on the subject.

There are no organizational changes, short of losing our jobs, that can compare on any level to emigrating from one country to another, with a family of four children and limited resources. All organizational change is trivial compared to emigration. We could place getting married, bringing children into the world and deciding to change our professions alongside emigration in the same category of significant change. These are changes that test who we are, and our determination and resilience.

Corporate reorganizations, new payroll systems, mergers, new products, markets and technologies are not as stressful as the personal changes mentioned above.

Webster's Dictionary defines change as 'to alter; to make different; to cause to pass from one state to another'. It's worth noting that Webster doesn't distinguish between 'personal' and 'organizational' change. There's an unstated implication hidden deep within that definition that 'change is change', regardless of the context.

There's something else worth mentioning at this point—the statement 'people resist change' is a statement about people, not about organizations. The way the statement is phrased is a tacit admission that it is a 'people response' issue—one that might be addressed better with the proper set of people skills or management skills.

The Webster definition acknowledges, without commentary, that 'change' is a generic term relating to a transition from an initial 'state' to a different 'state'.

If we embrace this notion that 'people resist change', then we have no choice but to factor this belief into how we manage our organizations. If tomorrow brings change, then we must change in order to survive. It doesn't matter what our organizations do, how they do it, where they do it or even why they do it; tomorrow will revalue current skills, processes and products, possibly to the point of obsolescence. Every organization knows that if we don't respond to the changes all around us, then the organization will fall behind the pack. Those that don't change no longer exist.

When we embrace the two beliefs—we must change in order to survive and people resist change—we decide that the way to bring change about is to tell people to change, since they won't do it voluntarily. And when we do this, we will, almost inevitably, encounter resistance to the change, reinforcing the core belief that people resist change and enticing us to redouble our efforts to force change onto the organization. Which, of course, causes people to resist more strongly.

We'll also decide to buy more books, attend more courses and sit in on more workshops in the hope that someone has the answer for overcoming resistance to change. We call this common cycle of behaviour a positive feedback loop.

When we decided that people resist change is a true statement, we ignored the hidden implication that change is change. Based on our experience as managers, we all certainly know that people resist change within our organizations. The problem is, in coming to that certain conclusion, we ignored how people respond to change outside of our organizations.

The personal changes that we mentioned earlier are usually extremely difficult to accomplish, and while we certainly take a lot of time deciding if we need to make them, we do choose to make them. We make these changes without anyone telling or forcing us to.

Which leads us to a possible useful question. Why do we embrace personal change and resist organizational change?

The answer is simple enough, even if it takes some effort to discover—autonomy, or at least a high level of involvement in the decision to change. Paul R. Lawrence, sociologist and professor of organizational behaviour at the Harvard Business School, noted in his article 'How to Deal with Resistance to Change', that 'the key to the problem is to understand the true nature of resistance'.[1]

Robert Tanner, founder and principal consultant of Business Consulting Solution, says 'people do not resist change that they believe is in their best interests'.[2]

Jim Collins, management consultant and author, notes in his bestseller *From Good to Great* that a lot of the executives interviewed by the researchers found the question about commitment, alignment, and how they managed change to be 'stupid'.[3]

Collins says that he and the researchers were astonished to find that 'the good-to-great companies paid scant attention to managing change, motivating people, or creating alignment'.

'Under the right conditions, the problems of commitment, alignment, motivation, and change largely melt away. They largely take care of themselves,' he writes.

While there are many answers in Collins's research, one is particularly notable because of its simplicity: 'lead with questions, not answers.' This meshes neatly with our experiences that dictated change generates resistance, while increased involvement and understanding diminishes it.

For any organizational change to succeed, the following are essential:

1. The objectives of the change should be well-defined, including end goals, the definition of success and the time-frame in which it should be completed. The more these objectives are generated in cooperation with those affected most by the change, the greater the level of engagement.
2. 'Change that is poorly communicated will only stir up organizational resistance,' says Tanner.[2] We agree. There must be communication to the team on the change, the need for it and the benefits from it. Invite suggestions and ideas for improving the programme. If not involved, the team will resist the change and correctly feel it is being forced or thrust on them. Communication must be ongoing throughout the change process, and no amount of it can ever be enough. When you have achieved this change, the entire team will have ownership of the change, and will have been a part of creating the idea. The change will belong to them as much as it does to the management.
3. Creating a team of 'champions' to sustain ongoing enthusiasm. These should be pulled from every category of stakeholders, which ensures that everyone is represented on the Change Team, and that one of their own is taking care of their interests. Change management consultant Jonathan Mills points out that 'appointing early adopters as change champions helps the organization with managing the inevitable ambiguity and uncertainty associated with implementing change'.[4]

4. Adequate training for the changing ways of working.
5. Defining milestones and a roadmap for the change, and measuring through the journey.
6. Examining structural and process changes required to make the initiative a success.

When you have implemented all the above well, you will be on the road to success. There will still be an issue of addressing the persons who lose out due to the change, as most changes will have several winners and a few losers. If we don't find alternate career paths for the 'losers' from the change, you may expect resistance to change. More dangerous is rampant sullenness, lack of motivation, disengagement and low morale. All this can affect organizational culture, leading to a toxic environment, which can then lead to a failure of the change.

T.T. Jagannathan, chairman of the TTK Group, a conglomerate with two publicly listed companies and businesses across thirty categories including kitchen appliances, food and pharma, had to contend with resistance to change when he took charge of TTK Prestige. He notes in his autobiography *Disrupt & Conquer* that when he was asked by his father to run the family's pressure cooker business (then known as TT Ltd), he faced intense hostility from the workers. The employees felt that profits were being used to prop up the group's other ailing companies, and worried that the new managing director would destroy the company.[5]

Jagannathan decided not to occupy the MD's office until he gained their trust. The workers' attitude began to change when he was successful in restarting production (it had stopped due to a shortage of aluminium, which used to be controlled by the government in those days). However, while the workers appreciated his efforts, they would not let him interfere with the design or manufacturing processes. They felt they knew more about the business than he did, and Jagannathan acknowledged that the workers were right. He was a gold medallist from IIT, had a master's degree from Cornell, and was the chairman's son, but he didn't know the manufacturing processes.

He began to work hard alongside the workers, and after two years, the employees requested him to move to the MD's office. He was then able to start a series of manufacturing inventions and innovations that, alongside organizational growth strategies, made TTK Prestige India's largest kitchen appliances company and the group's flagship.

My coauthor Ashok believes that people resist change only when the change management process is handled poorly. Ashok recalls how he handled a situation poorly, and how he learned from it to turn the situation around.

In 1973, when he was general manager of Usha Fans in Calcutta (as it was called then), the group chairman, Charat Ram, asked him to move at short notice to Hyderabad to become chief executive of Shriram Refrigeration, a company which had a negative net worth due to years of losses. Ashok arrived in Hyderabad to find that the company was in the midst of its three-year cycle of wage negotiations. Ashok called his leadership team and said he would like to propose to the union to forego a wage increase in view of the company's precarious situation. The manager in charge of the negotiations acquiesced without telling him that a commitment had already been made. This same manager had hoped to be made chief executive, and resented Ashok's arrival. When Ashok made this proposal to the union, they promptly walked out and gave a strike notice. Since the cash-starved company could ill-afford a work stoppage, Ashok capitulated to their demands.

He also realized his own mistake. He was a stranger who had not earned the trust of the team, and was asking them to make a sacrifice. Ashok soon learned that in the lunch canteen and other forums, this same aspiring CEO was spreading cynicism regarding the turnaround effort. Ashok took two steps. First, this manager was fired summarily. Simultaneously, Ashok began building trust with workers. Production incentive schemes were created, and cash organized to support the increased production. Most importantly, Ashok began a series of dialogues with the officers and workers to earn their trust. Within a year, the company returned to profitability, thanks to the cooperation and commitment of the workers, who no longer resisted the changes required. Another lesson for Ashok was that a crisis is a great opportunity to overcome resistance to change, but you must have a well-thought-out change management strategy.

Several initiatives that Ashok implemented helped revive the company, and the workers came around as they could see a future for themselves. When he visited the factory after twenty-five years, he had a heartwarming experience.

Most of the managers from his time had left, but most of the workers and union leaders were still there. Ashok recalls that when he reached the plant, the workers came out of every shop floor to greet him with garlands, recalling the golden years of Shriram Refrigeration under his leadership. And these were the same people who had gone on strike within a week of his arrival!

These examples demonstrate that people resist change only when it is poorly implemented. The right strategy will ensure resistance to change can be overcome, and change can even become a force multiplier.

Key Takeaways

- Change management strategy is essential to overcome resistance to change.
- The need for change must be communicated clearly, and trust built.
- Crisis is a great opportunity to implement change.

15

Firing the Bottom 10 Per Cent

Peter de Jager

During his term as CEO and executive chairman of General Electric (GE) from 1981 until his retirement in 2001, Jack Welch took the company from a market capitalization of twelve billion US dollars to a stunning 410 billion, a thirty-four-fold increase. In doing so, he earned his place in the upper echelon of notable CEOs. When such an individual reveals some of what he considered vital management strategies, it is prudent to pay attention.

The one we're going to explore is his controversial strategy of 'firing the bottom 10 per cent' of employees annually. 'Neutron Jack' was the sobriquet Welch earned for his successful, albeit aggressive, strategies—'fire the bottom 10 per cent', and 'rank and yank' or 'stack ranking' was just one of his management tactics. After his success in implementing this at GE, several companies followed suit, including Microsoft under Steve Ballmer.[1] Many others across industries adopted it.

Welch's legacy has come under fire in recent times, and a new book by *The New York Times* columnist David Gelles holds him responsible for all that's wrong with capitalism.[2]

In an article for *The New Yorker*, Malcolm Gladwell explores if Jack Welch was the greatest CEO of his day, or the worst.[3] Apart from what he describes as 'the moral impoverishment of Welch's era', Gladwell writes that 'Welch seemed to enjoy firing people'. 'It is quite possible, in fact, that no single corporate executive in history has fired as many people as Jack Welch did,' he states.

Ashok, the coauthor of this book, and Nandan Nilekani, co-founder and non-executive chairman of Infosys, are among those in complete disagreement with Welch's strategy. We elaborate on their reasons later in this essay.

The measurement that Welch considered was performance. As is always the case, the short form of 'fire the bottom 10 per cent' is an almost content-free summary of his thinking, and yet, some organizations take it at face value and are perhaps oblivious to his far more nuanced thought process.

Welch explained the finer details in one of his books *Jack: What I've Learned Leading a Great Company and Great People*. He says company employees fall into three broad categories of performers: the top 20 per cent are 'A' level performers, followed by 'B' level performers who make up 70 per cent, and then the remaining 10 per cent 'C' level performers, or underperformers.

If this breakdown feels familiar to you, it's because it is almost totally in synch with a broader concept. One with a long-established history dating back to 1895, proving once again that there is nothing new under the sun.

The 80/20 Rule

We know that concept today as the Pareto principle or more commonly, as the '80/20 rule'. While researching land ownership in Italy, economist Vilfredo Pareto observed that 80 per cent of the land was owned by only 20 per cent of the population. The rule has since found applications in a range of areas, including management and human resources.

We can summarize the rule as '80 per cent of outputs are generated by 20 per cent of the inputs'. This rather simple idea has consequences across all types of activities; for example, 80 per cent of profit is generated by 20 per cent of our product line, 80 per cent of accidents are caused by 20 per cent of drivers, or 80 per cent of our business is generated by 20 per cent of our customers.

In the 1940s, Joseph Juran, a prominent contributor in the field of operations management, boiled the idea down even further to something closer to an aphorism: 'the vital few and the trivial many'.[4] This suggested that we should pay more attention to the vital few and less to the trivial many, which again resonates well with Welch's 'fire the bottom 10 per cent'.

The Pareto principle is a core component of any time management strategy—that 80 per cent of our productivity is achieved by 20 per cent of our activities. This results in the inevitable question: what happens to our productivity if we focus all our activity on that 20 per cent (once we identify what those activities are), and cease paying attention to the 80 per cent of the activities, which are adding insignificantly to our productivity? Replace 'activities' with 'people', and we're once again very close to Welch's dictum.

It's worth commenting at this point that the numbers in the 80/20 rule are only approximations, and that the two numbers adding up to 100 is a mere coincidence, which is often the source of some confusion. It is entirely possible that 80 per cent of our sales are driven by a single customer, and the other 1,000 customers in our sales book make up the remaining 20 per cent of sales. In this case, we could restate the rule as 80/.001 rule, but we don't, because this is a unique case and changing it to be precise is confusing.

It's also worth noting that if our company is in this situation, then we're highly vulnerable to that single vital customer finding another supplier. That vulnerability also gives the vital customer the upper hand in any price negotiations.

With all of these observations supporting the basic concept of 'fire the bottom 10 per cent', why have we decided to include Welch's strategy as a management myth?

Before we answer that question, we must, in the interests of full disclosure, complicate things even further. We are strong proponents of identifying underperformers in an organization, and attempting to correct the performance issues. If you fail in that endeavour, we advocate that you then set about removing the problematic individuals from the organization, sooner rather than later. Organizations cannot afford the overhead of continuing to employ those who are not active contributors to future growth.

Even with this added complication, the simple 'fire the bottom 10 per cent' poses significant issues.

Setting Context

When Welch states we must 'fire the bottom 10 per cent', he's doing so within the context of his precisely defined 20/70/10 performance breakdown. When doing this, he doesn't bring our attention to the fact that the 20/70/10 proportions are the averages he's experienced over time. They, just like the figures in the 80/20 rule, are approximations.

He could just as easily have stated 'fire your underperformers', but that is, in many ways, stating the blatantly obvious. As an excellent communicator, Welch understands the psychology of how people hear and interpret what they hear. People tend to ignore obvious statements, so instead, he said the same thing differently—'fire the bottom 10 per cent'. Since that statement is a novel one, we pay attention to it, and repeat it.

While Welch achieved his goal of getting the attention of managers far and wide, he introduced a different type of communication problem. His original statement is true and is good advice: as long as the ratios of 20/70/10 hold true in your organization, then firing the bottom 10 per cent is exactly the same as firing the underperformers. If, however, the ratios in your organization are 25/72/3, then firing the bottom 10 per cent is not the same as firing the underperformers.

There is always a bottom 10 per cent in any company—that's how rankings work—but in the case of a 25/72/3 ratio, the bottom 10 per cent includes 3 per cent of underperformers and 7 per cent of the company's employees who are performers. Firing people who are performing makes no business sense.

At one point in my career, my team consisted of ten employees. With help from my mentor, I hired good people from the start. I treated them well, provided coaching constantly, and training when required, to remove whatever weaknesses were hampering their performance. They were all 'A' performers. My ratio was, therefore, 100/0/0.

Was there one individual who wasn't as good as the others? Of course there was. But the person in question wasn't underperforming; in fact, they were an A-level performer that any manager would have been happy to have on the team. So, I chose not to heed Welch's strategy, and decided that the person would not be fired, overriding any management rule enforced from the top.

At the heart of the issue is that some organizations, and many managers, see 'fire the bottom 10 per cent' as a quota they must achieve, and if the corporate culture has any leanings toward being a bureaucratic organization, then the bottom 10 per cent are fired regardless of their level of performance.

Even more disturbing is the case of a company with a 10/60/30 performance ratio. In this case, managers stop firing the underperforming individuals once they achieve their quota of 10 per cent, when in fact, they should fire all 30 per cent who are at the bottom.

There is a secondary effect that is perhaps even more troublesome than the firing of the wrong people (the performers in our first example), or not firing enough of the right people (the non-performers in our second example). That is what a quota-based implementation of Welch's idea does to corporate culture.

Organizations work best when its employees work together to achieve its goals. This is one of those blatantly obvious statements we mentioned earlier. If we introduce the rule where we're annually firing the bottom 10 per cent, then working together to make everyone better is no longer the best strategy, if you wish to remain in the organization. Increasing the performance level of those working with you puts your job at risk.

When new people are brought on board, why should anyone, especially those in the 'B' category of employees, do anything to help them ease into their new roles? Doing so merely increases the likelihood that in the next management purge, they will outperform you, and your reward for helping them perform would be to receive your notice of termination. Nothing personal; it's just the rule the company follows.

Welch's dictum is directly tied to the specific employee performance distribution ratio of 20/70/10 that he observed in his organization. If your observed ratio is the same, then by all means, follow it to the letter. But when your ratio is different, it's best to adjust his advice to suit your situation.

Breeding Fear

Nilekani, who is critical of Welch's management style, told us that the strategy of 'firing the bottom 10 per cent' creates a culture where 'everybody is constantly looking over their shoulder'.

'It is a culture where every person looks out for themselves. There's no teamwork, no collaboration, no trust. In today's world, especially with the kind of work we do, we need trust, teamwork, collaboration and a handshake. I would obviously counsel people who are not performing, and if people are really not performing, they may not have a role, but it has to be done in a much gentler manner,' he said in our conversations for this book.

The Dilbert comic strip perfectly captures the problem that's at the core of this precept. If you fire the bottom 10 per cent, that would automatically put someone else in the bottom 10 per cent each year.

Hema Ravichandar, a strategic HR adviser, told us that firing the bottom 10 per cent or 5 per cent is difficult for companies to practice consistently, and would vary depending on talent crunch and volume of business.

'Organizations should look at employees as valued assets rather than just a number,' she said. 'Shining the light on the bottom 10 per cent and encouraging them to quickly come up to speed definitely encourages a high-performance work ethic, and a management style that means business while demonstrating empathy.'

How to let go of employees has become a matter of discussion. Some organizations offer high compensations and follow the up or out policy,[5] which can be compared with fire the bottom 10 per cent. In several industries such as accounting, law and management consulting, associates who can't move up to the expected level within a specific time are asked to leave the organization. An evolved company does so in a gracious and fair manner, and retains the goodwill of the ex-employees.

Boosting Productivity

Ashok had the opportunity to interact with several senior leaders of GE organizations between 1990 and 2000 as customers of Wipro, and also when he was a director of Wipro-GE. He agrees with Nilekani's observations on the cultural aspects of the Jack Welch dictum, and the insecurity it creates in people across all levels. This is hardly the right way to bring out the best performance from the team, he says.

Ashok feels that 'fire the bottom 10 per cent' acquired the stature of a myth for two reasons. First, the message came from Jack Welch, and no one could dispute his success in his heyday. Secondly, leaders saw this as an easy way to upgrade talent in their organizations.

Ashok's view is that the essence of success is the continuous upgradation of talent. There are many ways to do this, and weeding out non-performers is only one part. If the percentage of non-performers is ten or higher, the organization needs to look at its talent acquisition practices.

He says the best way to upgrade your talent is to continuously coach and develop your leaders. You must help them develop new skills and capabilities. Here, you should give higher attention to developing your top 20 per cent, but you must take care not to ignore the rest of the organization. Everyone has the ability to improve, and we are dealing with human beings, not machines!

According to Ashok, specifying any ratio for firing, even if it is 2 per cent, is counterproductive. We must remember, people do develop and grow. They must be given that opportunity. Quite often, a person is an underperformer because they are in the wrong role. In such cases, Ashok would explore job rotations and performance improvement programmes. If none of the above worked, he would not hesitate to fire the person.

One criterion where he would not hesitate to apply the axe is in cases where the values of the person are in dissonance with the values of the organization—he would fire the person even if they were a top performer in terms of results.

Ashok remembers his entry into Shriram Refrigeration with a mandate to turn around the loss-making company. He found the business leader of one division was not a team worker, and also expressed cynicism about the turnaround efforts, thereby impacting the morale. The firing of this leader had a very salutary effect on the whole organization, which began to work cohesively to bring about the turnaround.

Paul B. Brown, a veteran journalist and author, writes in his column that 'leaders of small companies are often remarkably slow when dealing with employee productivity problems'.[6] 'That isn't good for the employee who is underperforming. And it is definitely not good for your organization,' he says. He suggests you need to take action 'if you have one or more employees who are not pulling their weight'. Several other commentators note that letting underperformers linger could actually affect the morale of the team, and in turn, reduce productivity.

Marc Effron, publisher of *Talent Quarterly* and president of The Talent Strategy Group, suggests that you should be firing the 'next 10 per cent'.[8] These are employees who have been delivering 'just enough' performance for years. The organization would benefit by replacing such employees at 'the same price with higher-quality talent, and with relative ease', he writes.

As Captain Hector Barbossa says in the movie *Pirates of the Caribbean: The Curse of the Black Pearl*, 'the (pirates') code is more what you'd call "guidelines" than actual rules'. This bit of sage advice, admittedly from a fictional character, is directly applicable not only to Welch's rule, but to all other management rules. We must adjust how we follow any management rule/ advice to fit our specific situation.

Key Takeaways

- Firing people as per a fixed percentage is demoralizing, destroys culture and is counterproductive.
- Before you fire, help the underperformers improve.
- Outright non-performers should be fired, but humanely.
- Upgrade your talent by focusing on the top 20 per cent.

16

People Leave People, Not Organizations

Ashok Soota

Like many of the myths in this book, the statement that 'people leave people, not organizations' came to be accepted as truth because many people repeated it in one form or another: in articles, blogs and HR conferences.

Take the following statement, for example, from Marcus Buckingham and Curt Coffman, in their book *First, Break All the Rules*. They say that 'people leave managers, not companies' and 'how long an employee stays in a company is determined by his relationship with his immediate supervisor'. Another sample from Brigette Hyacinth reads: 'Employees don't quit their jobs; they quit their boss!'[1]

We could go on with such examples. Our reason for taking umbrage with this statement is that it is based on an erroneous assumption that bosses are toxic, like the pointy-haired boss of the Dilbert comic strip. The strip is to be seen as what it is—a comic strip. However, it does spread cynicism and far worse feelings about managers. Hyacinth continues in her post that 'in days past, managers would focus on developing their employees. Today, they are more focused on self-promotion and securing their position'.

Just see the set of assumptions above. Have all managers suddenly transformed into hydra-headed monsters and self-serving persons who just focus on self-promotion instead of developing their teams, and all the many things they need to do to be successful?

Most writers on attrition cite negative reasons for the same. Though we have no empirical evidence, except our own experience and our observations of large, successful companies, we would say that almost half of the attrition in companies is almost just the nature of things. People will leave companies even when they love the company and its work culture, and have excellent relationships with their immediate superiors.

There are multiple reasons for this. First, as the pyramid narrows, there are seldom enough opportunities for growth for everyone; the experience people gain in a successful company can create a remarkably high market value for them. Some people just want the experience of working in multiple environments to enhance their learning. Finally, at times, certain skills will have an exploding demand, such as skills in digital technologies today, leading to a sharp increase in attrition.

Another reason we take umbrage with 'people leave people and not organizations' is that ignoring these ground realities can lead to blaming certain leaders, and will only worsen attrition. Judgements along these lines must be based on an analysis of the major reasons for attrition. This is a complex issue, and before we get into it, let us give you a fascinating example of attrition comparison in India's top two IT companies—Tata Consultancy Services (TCS) and Infosys, both of whom have crossed twenty billion US dollars in revenue today.

For many years, TCS's attrition rate has remained at about 60 per cent of Infosys. Furthermore, TCS's attrition rate has been less than half that of the industry, including many young and rapidly growing companies as well as large multinationals present in India, such as IBM, Accenture and Capgemini. The Tata company didn't have the highest pay scales in the industry, or a generous stock option scheme (Infosys was the company that first distributed stocks widely).

For over three decades, TCS was led by three excellent, professional CEOs, though the first, F.C. Kohli (rightly reputed as the father of the Indian software industry) reportedly ran the company with military discipline—hardly the environment in which you would expect software professionals to be wedded. Infosys, for most of this period, was led by two charismatic founder–entrepreneurs—N.R. Narayana Murthy and Nandan Nilekani—both of whom acquired iconic status in the industry.

Though TCS was the larger company, Infosys was long considered the flagship company of Indian IT, until recently, when some leadership succession changes led to faltering growth (there are indications that this is changing again after Nilekani's return as non-executive chairman). The point being made is that Infosys's higher attrition (compared to TCS) was not due to negative reasons. Infosys has always been a successful company with an excellent culture and excellent leaders, but TCS seems to have a secret glue that has kept its team better bonded and intact over the years.

It is not that people don't quit because of bad, often toxic, managers. They obviously do. It's that the observation is offered as the only reason people quit their positions. As the statement stands, 'people quit managers and not organizations' is blatantly false. We quit both bad managers and bad organizations; we also quit for a vast variety of other reasons that have nothing to do with either our managers or our organizations.

To gather some current feedback on this topic, we polled our circle of associates, and asked them if the reason they quit their last position had more to do with their organization or their immediate manager. While many loved their managers and organizations, some negative responses we received are given below.

- Two years before I quit, my supervisor (who was great, by the way, and is today the president of the company and still a good friend) was promoted. His replacement, in my opinion, was a snake who:
    1. Took all the credit for team successes.
    2. Looked for a scapegoat when something went wrong.
    3. Played favourites.

- I quit my boss because:
    1. He was not trustworthy.
    2. He did not carry through on his promises.
    3. Kept changing what he said as time went on.
    4. When a decision turned out to be wrong, he denied giving the direction for it.

- I quit because I had a lack of trust in my manager, due to:
    1. Bullying and lack of integrity—plus, it was unsafe psychologically.
    2. The leadership not living up to the values it articulated.

- I quit my boss—he was a bully and has since been let go.

The last comment we listed is important, as it suggests there is a perfectly good solution to the real problem of toxic managers. A good organization must be on the lookout for such individuals—exit interviews are a proven way of identifying the bad apples in an otherwise good organization. Once the problem is identified, counselling and feedback are provided to the problematic manager. If that fails? Then the manager is shown the door. Having people leave good organizations because of a toxic manager isn't a sustainable business practice.

Putting aside reasons for leaving that have nothing to do with managers or the organization (health, career change, family issues, among others) we believe that the top reasons for attrition are as follows:

1. The organization's business results are below par and behind industry peers. In effect, nothing succeeds like success.
2. A toxic culture (not due to individual bosses) can be brought about by multiple reasons, such as dysfunctional competition between business units, impacting collaboration.
3. Lack of transparency, trust and empowerment. For low attrition, an organization must be seen as a 'great place to work'.[2]
4. Differences in belief systems between the organization and the employee, such as political, social, ethical and environmental. While these were not as prominent a few decades ago, there is a rising trend for people to align themselves with organizations that share their beliefs, or at least, don't work against the beliefs of the individual.
5. Poor HR processes and practices such as erratic appraisal/feedback mechanism, inadequate focus on well-being and health, no culture of fun, and inadequate reward and recognition.

6. Finally, compensation-related reasons, including the absence of widespread stock option schemes or profit-sharing.

It will be noted that all the major reasons listed by us for high attrition are attributable to an organization, as distinct from individual pointy-haired bosses, a la Dilbert. A proper analysis of the root cause for attrition will lead to the creation of a healthier company. Attrition will never come down to zero or near zero, for reasons which we described as in the 'nature of things'. However, there is no reason why you, dear reader, can't bring your attrition levels down to best-in-class in your own industry, and among your comparable peers. Especially since one of the easiest problems for a good organization to solve is that of the pointy-haired boss.

Didier Elzinga, founder and CEO of Culture Amp, terms the belief that 'people leave bosses and not organizations' as the 'biggest lie in HR'.[3]

'Yes, people leave bad managers, but it is not the number one reason people leave a company. In "good" companies, managers make a difference. In "bad" companies, good or bad managers make little to no difference to a person's decision to leave,' he says, summarizing a study.

We spoke with Hema Ravichandar, strategic HR adviser, about this issue. 'It is very true that people do leave leaders, especially managers. A bad manager could be one who is not inclusive as a leader, not communicative enough or lacks a good balance of empathy and strategy. All of these can lead to people leaving. Even when employees leave for other reasons, such as higher pay or better work, a good manager can ensure that people see the opportunities that lie ahead and encourage people to stay,' she said.

However, according to Ravichandar, it would be unfair and simplistic to make the manager the only scapegoat for why people quit. Employees may choose to leave to explore entrepreneurship when they feel that an organization doesn't have a strong purpose, or if they experience a mismatch of values between the organization and themselves, or if they feel that the current job is not interesting enough, or doesn't offer enough learning opportunities anymore.

Here, I can cite the example of a person who left a multinational IT company to come back to work for Happiest Minds. 'It wasn't just the money; I felt there were more opportunities to grow in my old company and my old boss, who I like and admire, called me back,' this employee said. This small recollection sums up the reality of why we sometimes decide to leave an organization—humans are motivated to leave by a complex combination of reasons. In this case, the personal connection with the old boss, and the financial and career prospects, combined to present an offer that they simply couldn't refuse. This job switch happened before the pandemic upended the world as we knew it.

Sometimes people will leave, no matter what. Your organization might be the best at what it does, with model HR practices, and you might be an exemplary leader. People will still leave. We suggest you don't beat yourself up about it. When people leave, and they will, it's worth noting the words of John Maxwell, the New York Times No.1 bestselling author, coach, and speaker. The question, he says, is not 'are people leaving?'. It is, 'who is leaving?'.

It would serve organizations well to note his conclusion: not everyone will take the journey with you. Not everyone should take the journey with you. Not everyone can take the journey with you.

Postscript: How COVID-19 Changed Things

COVID-19 brought in its wake turbulence in the job market which was called the Great Resignation. Across the world and across industries, there's a shortage of talent and resources as people seem to be quitting their jobs in droves—2.9 per cent of the entire American workforce quit in 2021, while a staggering 86 per cent of talent in Indian corporates were slated to seek new jobs in 2022.[4]

We hear the alarm bells ringing about the Great Resignation, and are convinced that it's not the individual bosses at fault. Analysing the phenomenon of record numbers of American employees voluntarily quitting their jobs, Joseph Fuller and William Kerr note in an article in the *Harvard Business Review* that 'what we are living through is not just short-term turbulence provoked by the pandemic. Instead, it's the continuation of a trend of rising quit rates that began more than a decade ago'.

They identify 'Five Rs' that have combined to yield the changes in the US labour market: 'retirement, relocation, reconsideration, reshuffling, and reluctance'.

'Workers are retiring in greater numbers, but aren't relocating in large numbers; they're reconsidering their work–life balance and care roles; they're making localized switches among industries, or reshuffling, rather than exiting the labor market entirely; and, because of pandemic-related fears, they're demonstrating a reluctance to return to in-person jobs,' they write.

Some of the same reasons hold good in India. Stores don't have staff; delivery companies are running short of agents; and factories don't have enough workers. Much of this is because the workforce, to a large extent, comprises domestic migrants, who have gone back to their villages or towns and don't have the incentive to return to the big cities. A *Fortune India* report attributes the reluctance to 'the trauma of distress migration of 2020, low wages, lack of social security and support systems' in urban areas, which have combined to reduce the return of migrant workers.[5] The report quotes staffing solution provider TeamLease, which estimates that there is a shortage of 15–25 per cent of workers across industries, particularly in manufacturing, engineering, construction, healthcare and pharmaceuticals.

A report in the *Deccan Herald* quotes Lohit Bhatia, president of workforce management at Quess Corp Limited, as saying that attrition in India's IT industry, which employs 4.5 million people, is 25–35 per cent.[6] Companies are feeling the talent crunch acutely, as the pandemic has driven all businesses to boost their IT, tech transformation and digital initiatives. Retail, manufacturing, hospitality, startups, edutech and fintech are also facing high attrition rates.

Naman HR, a management-consulting firm, conducted 'The Great Resignation Survey 2022', and concluded that four out of every ten employees wanted to resign from their current organizations post-increment; six out of every ten male workers were planning to resign, and one out of ten of those who planned to quit wanted to start their own businesses. The three sectors in which a majority of workers reported contemplating resignation were service (37 per cent), manufacturing (31 per cent), and IT (27 per cent). Interestingly, the survey notes that 'only 15 per cent of employees surveyed feel that their decision to leave an organization is driven by the discomfort with their reporting manager'.[7]

Are employees leaving because they want a better work–life balance? Are they afraid to return to offices because of the fear of the pandemic? Do they want higher pay because of inflation and the increased cost of living? Do they want to become entrepreneurs or stay-at-home parents? There are varied reasons for employees to quit. Organizations can't have a one-size-fits-all policy to retain or attract talent. They will need to evolve flexible and specific responses to power their growth.

Key Takeaways

- People will leave despite good leadership, robust HR practices and an excellent culture.
- Toxic managers do contribute to attrition and it's best to show them the door.
- You can't stop attrition, but you must focus on who's leaving. Do your best to retain your future leaders.

17

You Should Hire People Smarter Than Yourself

ASHOK SOOTA

When I started my latest venture, Happiest Health, in 2021, it was undoubtedly a challenge for me to make time for it, as I have a very demanding day job as the chairman of Happiest Minds, apart from several other non-profit initiatives with which I am involved. The advice I got to run this new company, which was in a very different domain, was 'hire someone smarter than you'. But I decided not to look for a CEO immediately. I had already begun assembling a team, and we proceeded to spend a year or so exploring the way forward in the new vertical. How this played out will be clearer later in this chapter!

The last time we heard of someone notable who hired someone he thought was smarter than himself was Steve Jobs bringing John Sculley into Apple in 1983. We are also familiar with the aftermath: in 1985, Sculley secured the board's support to take away Steve Jobs's executive powers, leading to the latter's resignation. Fortunately, this story had a happy ending, because a wiser Steve Jobs returned years later to make Apple the most valuable company in the world.

How did 'hire people smarter than yourself' become a widely accepted example of 'good advice'? Obviously, many people endorse this approach, with or without qualifications. Here's a sample quote from pharmaceutical entrepreneur Ewing Marion Kauffman: 'Hire people who are smarter than you! In doing so, you prevent limiting the organization to the level of your own ability—and you grow the capabilities of your company. If you hire people you consider smarter than you, you are more likely to listen to their thoughts and ideas, and this is the best way to expand on your own capabilities and build the strength of your company.'[1]

Others justify the statement by saying it's necessary to upgrade the quality of your talent.

Unfortunately, both of these are examples of non-sequitur reasoning.

It is not that there is no value in the concept as stated. It should, and would, be of much use in the instances of insecure or underconfident managers. Some managers are threatened by those who challenge them. This category of managers exists within most organizations.

Some managers, usually those new to the role of managing and leading others in pursuit of a goal, don't feel comfortable with a team that questions their management decisions. To this category of managers, the advice to 'hire people smarter than you' has more than a little bit of merit, though it might be better framed as 'don't rely only on your expertise when making decisions, seek input from others, and then decide.'

There's the added consideration that even when this category of managers does happen to hire those 'smarter' than themselves, they fail, in that they refuse to learn from the new hires. Hiring good people fails as a strategy if it's not combined with an openness to consider new ideas.

There are a lot of managers—too many of them to be honest—who don't respond well to questions, challenges and differing opinions. The best advice to them is: open yourself up to new ideas; you can create a good source of those ideas by hiring those who are more knowledgeable than yourself.

When people say 'hire people smarter than you', they mostly seem to be referring to the IQ of the person. Bill Gates reportedly placed great importance on hiring persons with high IQ.

I met Gates during his first visit to India in March 1997. Immediately after he met with Prime Minister Vajpayee, he met with Azim Premji and me (I was leading Wipro Infotech at the time and Premji was the chairman). Gates posed sharp, probing questions in a rapid-fire manner for an hour on what technology solutions Wipro was offering. So probing were these questions that I had to reply at least twice that I would need to check that one out! It would be fair to assume that Gates didn't find too many (or maybe even a single person) smarter than himself.

Brilliant leaders/managers do face challenges in trying to find and hire smart people. However, those who focus on IQ when they talk of hiring someone smarter than themselves ignore the concept of multiple intelligences, first articulated by Howard Gardner in 1983. These include spatial, linguistic, mathematical, interpersonal and intrapersonal intelligence. This also led to the concept of emotional intelligence and EQ.

With my years of experience as a CEO in various companies, I undoubtedly find it very hard to find a replacement who has the same amount of accumulated wisdom. To point out yet another pitfall, should a finance manager hire someone smarter than themselves as a deputy? If such a thing were to happen, in all likelihood, the deputy would want the manager's job in a year, leaving the CEO to deal with a troublesome choice.

It is, of course, not our case that you should not be looking to hire smart people. However, equally important are knowledge, experience, aptitude for learning and values. The new hire should have the potential to be as good as, or better than, the incumbent. The phrase 'hire people smarter than yourself' fails if 'smarter' only means 'smarter' with respect to an IQ score. It is terrible advice if and only if the definition of 'smarter' is restricted to raw intelligence, and does not take into account desirable outcomes. Nobody cares, or at least we shouldn't care, if someone is 'smart'; we care if people can deliver what we specifically hire them to deliver.

Let's shift the emphasis to hiring someone who might not necessarily be smarter than you but has more knowledge about aspects that you don't have. You should always seek to hire someone from whom you can learn a lot more than you already know.

For example, if we are seeking to hire a CFO, we would acknowledge their functional expertise, and should be able to learn from them every day.

Hopefully, we would also be able to add value by adding a broader perspective.

Likewise, if the CFO is looking for a taxation specialist, they would seek to find someone who knows taxation issues in greater depth. In effect, we need to look for people better at their jobs than we can be. We need to hire those who are more knowledgeable than ourselves in the areas where we know, or suspect, that we have a deficit.

There is the principle of complementary hiring. Let's assume that you require A and B knowledge or skills for your role, and you are strong in A but weak in B. When you hire, look for someone strong in B, and you will make a more complete team. There's little point in hiring people who know as much as you do about the same subject, those whose skill sets mirror yours.

We spoke with Revathy Ashok, co-founder of Strategy Garage, a strategy and growth consulting firm. '"Hiring people smarter than you" is about being extremely self-aware of what you don't know, and filling the gap with people that have the knowledge that you lack,' she said.

That knowledge would change with time, she pointed out. 'You start your business at a certain stage, and are successful in building a minimum viable product, getting the first customer, etc. But what got you here may not get you there. I think the ability to understand this is very critical. The people you hire need not be vertically smarter than you. They could have lateral knowledge about things that you don't know,' she added.

Perhaps you are a scientist, but need to hire a scientist with very specific skills that you might not possess. 'One way to overcome any reluctance you might feel is to be secure in where you are and who you are,' Revathy Ashok said. 'I have to emphasize and reemphasize that the point is not just getting in people. You can feel secure about getting these people because you know how to use this input from all these people. You are getting them to fill various gaps, but you are the one who can string the pearls better than anybody else can in the team.'

A lot hinges on mutual respect, Revathy Ashok added. 'You must choose the right people with the right skills and attitude, and make sure that the people that you work with respect you for what you bring to the table, as much as you respect them for what they bring to the table. When you bring people who you think are smarter than you in certain ways, they must also believe that you are equally smart in certain other ways, and then there will be that feeling of mutual respect.'

What you should do is surround yourself with those who know more than you in as many areas as possible. Become the prime integrator of those ideas that you, through wise hiring decisions, have made available to your decision-making process.

The CEO needs a team that's collectively smarter than them, with each functional head being smarter than the CEO in their individual functions. When I was hired as the CEO of Wipro, I had no idea about IT, as I came from the manufacturing industry. But the day I joined Wipro, one of the first things I did was seek out Sridhar Mitta, the chief technical officer, and ask for his help in understanding the technology. I wanted to work with a functional head who was smarter than me to do all that was required to make Wipro a successful technology company.[2]

Another angle with which to approach this question is that you should hire people who are not just smart, but also strong. By this, we mean people who can take a stand against you, and confidently recommend approaches for action that are contrary to your own preference. I always remember Azim Premji as a person who looked for strong leaders, ones who had the courage of their convictions.

Another approach that will ensure that you have smart people in your organization is to help your people become 'smarter'. It is your responsibility to provide growth paths to your team members. It is important to remember here that an outstanding manager in one role may not be successful in a different or higher role. This is because the key factors for success in the next role will probably be dramatically different from the requirements which contributed to the person's success in the earlier role. During this period, you should give all your team members opportunities to acquire new skills and experiences.

Coming back to my reason for not appointing a CEO right away for Happiest Health, I wanted to wait until the company had gained traction. While I was clear about the company's philosophy of kinder, gentler therapies, the philosophy was still evolving, and I felt it would have been hard to find someone who shared it equally. In its early stage, I was also keen on defining the mission, vision and values of Happiest Health to reflect my philosophy and years of experience. So, I focused on hiring the best functional heads instead, to benefit from the collective intelligence of the team.

Over a year after the company was established, we got an excellent CEO, Anindya Chowdhury. He is smarter than me in terms of his 'business to consumer' knowledge and experience. He also acknowledges the breadth and depth of my experience. This leads to the mutual respect that Revathy Ashok talks about, and is propelling Happiest Health into a high growth path.

Intelligence is a power source—when combined with knowledge, and then directed towards a goal, it's an unstoppable juggernaut. By itself, in isolation, it's merely disruptive, rarely delivering a positive outcome. When you are ready to vacate your role, you will hopefully have groomed your successor. You will have done the right thing for your organization and your team if your successor is smarter, stronger and more empathetic than you for their new job. If you are not yet ready to move on from your role, we would certainly not recommend that you look for someone smarter than yourself, a la Steve Jobs!

Postscript: Peter says it can be argued though that Jobs's error was that Sculley wasn't actually 'smarter' than Jobs, but demonstrably more ambitious, more political, and believed he knew more than Jobs about how to move Apple forward.

Sculley was perhaps a victim of Dunning-Kruger,[3] where a little knowledge is a weakness that leads us to believe we know more than we actually do. He believed he was smarter than Jobs, but in actuality, he was incapable of delivering.

Key Takeaways

- To hire 'smarter' think of multiple intelligences and complementary skills.
- All hires must be more knowledgeable than you in their functional area of expertise. You must have the capability to add value to them. A CEO should lead a team that's collectively smarter than them.
- Each successor in a role—be they a CEO or a CFO—should be smarter than the predecessor.

Notes

Preface

1 Michael E. Porter, 'What Is Strategy?', *Harvard Business Review*, November–December 1996. https://hbr.org/1996/11/what-is-strategy

Part 1: Busting Myths about Strategy

1: Culture Eats Strategy for Breakfast

1 Rick Torben, 'Organizational Culture Eats Strategy for Breakfast, Lunch and Dinner', *Meliorate*, 11 June 2014. https://www.torbenrick.eu/blog/ culture/organisational-culture-eats-strategy-for-breakfast-lunch- and-dinner/
2 Zoë Corbyn, 'Why Sexism Is Rife in Silicon Valley', *The Observer*, 17 March 2018. https://wwwtheguardian.com/world/2018/mar/17/sexual-harassment-silicon-valley-emily-chang-brotopia-interview
3 Alexander DiLeonardo, Ran Li Phleps and Brooke Weddle, 'Establish a Performance Culture as Your "Secret Sauce"', McKinsey & Company, 27 July 2020. https://www.mckinsey.com/capabilities/people-and-

organizational-performance/our-insights/the-organization-blog/establish-a-performance-culture-as-your-secret-sauce

4 LDRFA, 'Cisco CEO John Chambers Turns Dyslexia into Strength', 4 October 2019. https://www.ldrfa.org/how-john-chambers-struggled-with-dyslexia-and-became-the-ceo-of-cisco/Ashok remembers another interaction with Chambers at a session that I was hosting for the Confederation of Indian Industry. Chambers was the scheduled speaker and shortly before the event, he asked me what the audience would like to hear about, and I mentioned three points. He asked me to repeat them, figuratively marking the points on his fingers—being dyslexic, he was internalizing the three points. And then he went on to amplify them into an electrifying speech.

5 CaseReads, 'Case Study of Reliance: An Unconventional Diversification Story', 20 August 2020. https://casereads.com/case-study-of- reliance-an-unconventional-diversification-story/

2: The Essence of Strategy Is Choosing What Not to Do

1 Mary Hanbury, 'Bill Gates Says His "Greatest Mistake Ever" Was Failing to Create Android at Microsoft', *Business Insider*, 24 June 2019. https://www.businessinsider.in/bill-gates-says-his-greatest-mistake-ever-was-failing-to-create-android-at-microsoft/articleshow/69926096.cms

3: It's Lonely at the Top

1 Manfred F. R. Kets De Vries, 'The Cure for the Loneliness of Command', Management-Issues.Com, 18 March 2019. https://www.management-issues.com/opinion/7341/the-cure-for-the-loneliness-of-command/

2 Thomas J. Saporito, 'It's Time to Acknowledge CEO Loneliness', *Harvard Business Review*, 15 February 2012. https://hbr.org/2012/02/its-time-to-acknowledge-ceo-lo

3 Training Industry, 'Size of the Training Industry', 29 March 2021, *Training Industry*. https://tr ainingindustr y.com/wiki/lear ning-ser vices-and- outsourcing/size-of-training-industry/

4 Chris Westfall, 'Leadership Development Is a $366 Billion Industry: Here's Why Most Programs Don't Work', *Forbes*, 20 June 2019. https://www.forbes.com/sites/chriswestfall/2019/06/20/leadership-development-why-most-programs-dont-work/

5 Jena McGregor, 'Tim Cook, the Interview: Running Apple "Is Sort of a Lonely Job"', *Washington Post*, 13 August 2016. http:// www.washingtonpost.com/sf/business/2016/08/13/tim-cook-the-interview-running-apple-is-sort-of-a-lonely-job/

6 Stefan Stern and Cary Cooper. *Myths of Management: What People Get Wrong about Being the Boss.* United Kingdom: Kogan Page, 2017.

7 Marion M. Chamberlain, 'One of the Biggest Leadership Myths: It's Lonely at the Top', 1 March 2016. https://www.linkedin.com/pulse/one-biggest-leadership-myths-its-lonely-top-marion-chamberlain-coker

8 Adam Waytz, Eileen Chou, Joe Magee and Adam Galinsky. 'Not Lonely at the Top', *The New York Times*, 24 July 2015, opinion section. https://www.nytimes.com/2015/07/26/opinion/not-lonely-at-the-top.html

9 Roger M. Schwarz, *Smart Leaders, Smarter Teams: How You and Your Team Get Unstuck to Get Results.* Germany: Wiley, 2013.

10 Jena McGregor, 'Tim Cook, the Interview: Running Apple "Is Sort of a Lonely Job"', https://www.washingtonpost.com/sf/business/2016/08/13/tim-cook-the-interview-running-apple-is-sort-of-a-lonely-job/

11 Manfred F. R. Kets de Vries. 'The Cure for the Loneliness of Command', *INSEAD Knowledge*, 14 March 2019. https://knowledge.insead.edu/leadership-organisations/cure-loneliness-command

12 Silvia Pencak, 'It's Lonely at the Top', PLC, 18 September 2017. https://silviapencak.com/lonely-at-the-top/

13 John C. Maxwell, *Leadership Gold: Lessons I've Learned from a Lifetime of Leading.* United States: HarperCollins Leadership, 2008.

4: Fail Fast, Fail Cheap

1 Quote Fancy, 'Top 200 Michael Jordan Quotes', https://quotefancy.com/michael-jordan-quotes

2 'Fail Fast, Fail Cheap, and Fail *often*!!', *The Clever PM*, 25 August 2015. http://www.cleverpm.com/2015/08/25/fail-fast-fail-cheap- and-fail-often/

3 Rose Leadem, 'When It Makes Sense to Release an Imperfect Product', *Entrepreneur*, 30 May 2017.

4 Meha Agarwal, '[What The Financials] with No Monetisation Plan in Place Till 2020, Hike Messenger May Just Have to Go Take a Hike', *Inc42 Media*, 17 August 2018. https://inc42.com/datalab/

with-no-monetising-plan-in-place-till-2020-hike-messenger-may-just-have-to-go-take-a-hike/

5 Ananya Bhattacharya, qz.com. 'Once Considered India's Answer to WhatsApp, Hike Messenger Has Shut Down', *Scroll.in*, 21 January2021. https://scroll.in/article/984580/once-considered-indias- answer-to-whatsapp-hike-messenger-has-shut-down

6 Sushma UN, 'An Indian Unicorn Admits It Screwed Up and Is Rebooting with Layoffs', *Quartz*, 30 May 2018. https://qz.com/india/1291412/kavin-bharti-mittals-hike-admits-losing-focus-and-is-now-rebooting-with-layoffs

7 'Hike Shows Why Super Apps Don't Work in India the Way They Do in China', Greyhound Research, 16 January 2019. https://greyhoundresearch.com/hike-shows-why-super-apps-dont-work-in-india-the-way-they-do-in-china/

8 Doug White and Polly. '4 Times "Fail Fast, Fail Cheap" Is the Wrong Advice', *Entrepreneur*, 24 May 2017. https://www.entrepreneur.com/growing-a-business/4-times-fail-fast-fail-cheap-is-the-wrong-advice/294308

9 Andrea Huspeni. 'Why Mark Zuckerberg Runs 10,000 Facebook Versions a Day', *Entrepreneur*, 24 May 2017. https://www.entrepreneur.com/science-technology/why-mark-zuckerberg-runs-10000-facebook-versions-a-day/294242

10 Stephen McCranie, https://www.stephenmccranie.com/books

11 The Decision Lab, 'Why Are We Likely to Continue with an Investment Even If It Would Be Rational to Give It Up?', https://thedecisionlab.com/biases/the-sunk-cost-fallacy

12 Aytekin Tank, 'James Dyson Created 5,127 Versions of a Product That Failed before Finally Succeeding. His Tenacity Reveals a Secret of Entrepreneurship', *Entrepreneur*, 23 May 2022. https://www.entrepreneur.com/leadership/james-dyson-created-5127-versions-of-a-product-that-failed/424645

13 Debojyoti Ghosh and Fortune India. 'The Gold Rush for India's SuperApp', Fortune India, 10 February 2022. https:// www.for tuneindia.com/long-reads/the-gold-r ush-for-indias-superapp/107066

5: Early Adopter

1 Harshit Rakheja, 'Indian OTT Industry Poised for Growth. But Are Low Prices Sustainable?', *Business Standard*, 4 January 2022, Current Affairs Section. https://www.business-standard.com/podcast/

current-affairs/indian-ott-industry-poised-for-growth-but-are-low-prices-sustainable-122010400106_1.html

2 'OTT Penetration Stands at 27%, Hotstar Is the Preferred Choice for a Majority of the OTT Viewers: Report', Business Insider India, 1 December 2021. https://www.businessinsider.in/advertising/brands/article/ott-penetration-stands-at-27-hotstar-is-the-preferred-choice-for-a-majority-of-the-ott-viewers-report/articleshow/88024131.cms

3 'Deloitte's 2022 TMT Predictions for India: Press Release', Deloitte India, 22 February 2022. https://www2.deloitte.com/in/en/pages/technology-media-and-telecommunications/articles/big-bets-on-smartphones-semiconductors-and-streaming-service.html

4 Vignesh Anantharaj, 'India Has Adopted Latest and Best Tech Ahead of Others', *Mint*, 21 February 2022. https://www.livemint. com/companies/people/india-has-adopted-latest-and-best-tech- ahead-of-others and 11645457976634.html

5 F. Floyd. Shoemaker and Everett M. Rogers, *Communication of Innovations: A Cross-Cultural Approach.* United Kingdom: Free Press, 1971.

6 Rahul Awati, 'Early Adopter', https://www.techtarget.com/searchitoperations/definition/early-adopter

7 Niccolò Machiavelli, *The Prince.* United States: Dante University Press, 2002.

8 Linda Rising. 'Myths and Patterns of Organizational Change', BCoaching, 13 November 2021. https://bcoaching.online/myths-and-patterns-of-organizational-change/

9 Muntazir Abbas. 'Jio-Led Data Price Reduction Fuels Smartphone Adoption in India: Cisco', *The Economic Times*, 28 June 2018. https://economictimes.indiatimes.com/industry/telecom/telecom-news/jio-led-data-price-reduction-fuels-smartphone-adoption-in-india-cisco/articleshow/64774860.cms

Part 2: Busting Myths about Process

6. Best Practices

1. Michael Hammer, 'Reengineering Work: Don't Automate, Obliterate', *Harvard Business Review*, from the Magazine (July–August 1990), https://hbr.org/1990/07/reengineering-work-dont-automate-obliterate; Thomas H. Davenport and James E. Short, 'The New

Industrial Engineering: Information Technology and Business Process Redesign', *MIT Sloan Management Review,* 15 July 1990, https://sloanreview.mit.edu/article/the-new-industrial- engineering-information-technology-and-business-process-redesign/;MichaelHammer and James Champy, 'Reengineering the Corporation: A Manifesto for Business Revolution', HarperCollins Publishers, 1993, https://www.harpercollins.com/ products/reengineering-the-corporation-michael-hammerjames- champy?variant=32117134721058

2 Art Kleiner, 'Revisiting Reengineering', 1 July 2000, *Strategy+Business* (a PWC publication), https://www.strategy-business.com/article/19570

3 Merriam Webster, https://www.merriam-webster.com/dictionary/best%20practice

4 Peter F. Drucker, *Management: Tasks, Responsibilities, Practices,* Routledge, 1974

5 Dilbert comic strip

6 Jacque Vilet, 'The Myth of Best Practices: They Lead to Conformity, or Worse', TLNT, 4 February 2014. https://www.tlnt.com/the-myth- of-best-practices-they-lead-to-conformity-or-worse/

7 Diane Edwards, 'The Myth of Best Practice', 1 March 2019. https://www.linkedin.com/pulse/myth-best-practice-diane-edwards

8 Mike Myatt, 'Best Practices—Aren't', *Forbes,* 15 August 2012, https://www.forbes.com/sites/mikemyatt/2012/08/15/best-practices-arent/

9 Diego Piacentini, 'The Myth of Best Practices', *Stanford ECorner,* 3 November 2010. https://ecorner.stanford.edu/clips/the-myth-of-best-practices/

10 Harsimran Julka. 'Amazon Sets up Logistics Company in India to Deliver Products Directly to Clients', *The Economic Times,* 24 March 2015. https://economictimes.indiatimes.com/industry/services/retail/amazon-sets-up-logistics-company-in-india-to-deliver-products-directly-to-clients/articleshow/46668915.cms?from=mdr

7: Automate Everything

1 Soumya Chatterjee, 'A Bike Rental Company in Bengaluru Is Allowing Many to Sustain on Delivery Work', *The News Minute,* 23 August 2021. https://www.thenewsminute.com/article/bike-rental-company-bengaluru-allowing-many-sustain-delivery-work-154271

2 'No Driving License? No Problem!', *Yulu*, 5 August 2021. https://www.yulu.bike/blogposts/no-driving-license-no-problem/

3 Dominic Gates, 'Final Report on Boeing 737 MAX Crash Sparks Dispute Over Pilot Error', 6 January 2023, *Seattle Times*, https://www.seattletimes.com/business/boeing-aerospace/final-report-on-boeing-737-max-crash-disputed-agencies-note-pilot-error-as-a-factor/; Dominic Gates, 'International Regulator Report Slams Boeing, FAA Over 737 MAX Design and Approval', 11 October 2019, *Seattle Times*, https://www.seattletimes.com/business/boeing-aerospace/international-regulator-report-slams-boeing-faa-over-737-max-design-and-approval/

4 'Automation Professional Services', *ThinkAutomation*. https://www.thinkautomation.com/professionalservices

5 Daron Acemoglu and Pascual Restrepo, 'The Revolution Need Not Be Automated', *Project Syndicate*, 29 March 2019. https://www.project-syndicate.org/commentary/ai-automation-labor-productivity-by-daron-acemoglu-and-pascual-restrepo-2019-03

8: If It Ain't Broke, Don't Fix It

1 Seim Mol, '6 Major Companies That Failed to Innovate in Time', *Ground Control*, 7 October 2020. https://togroundcontrol.com/blog/6- major-companies-that-failed-to-innovate-in-time/

2 Dave P, 'What the Rise and Fall of the Ambassador Teaches about Business', *The Story Watch*, 14 March 2021. https://thestorywatch.com/what-the-rise-and-fall-of-the-ambassador-teaches-about-business/

3 Jennifer Aaker and Victoria Chang, 'Obama and the Power of Social Media and Technology', Stanford Graduate School of Business, 27 August 2009. https://www.gsb.stanford.edu/faculty-research/case-studies/obama-power-social-media-technology

9: PowerPoint-Type Presentations Are Boring

1 Geoffrey James, 'Jeff Bezos Banned PowerPoint and It's Arguably the Smartest Management Move He's Ever Made', Inc.com, 25 October 2019. https://www.inc.com/geoffrey-james/jeff-bezos-banned-powerpoint-its-arguably-smartest-management-move-that-hes-ever-made.html

2 Paul Armstrong, 'Stop Using PowerPoint, Harvard University Says It's Damaging Your Brand and Your Company', *Forbes*, 5 July 2017. https://www.forbes.com/sites/paularmstrongtech/2017/07/05/stop-using-powerpoint-harvard-university-says-its-damaging-your-brand-and-your-company/

3 Emma Groeneveld, 'Lascaux Cave', World History Encyclopedia, 6 September 2016. https://www.worldhistory.org/Lascaux_Cave/.

4 'Is PowerPoint Dead?', Corporate Events London, UK, 8 August 2018. https://corporate-events.co.uk/is-powerpoint-dead/

5 Anett Grant, 'PowerPoint Isn't Dead Yet: Three Presentation Tips That Still Work in 2017', *Fast Company*, 14 January 2017. https://www.fastcompany.com/3067024/powerpoint-isnt-dead-yet-three-presentation-tips-that-still-work-in-2017

6 Bruce Murray, '5 Ways to Avoid Death by PowerPoint Presentation', *Mind Tools*, 19 October 2017. https://www.mindtools.com/blog/5-ways-to-avoid-death-by-powerpoint-presentation/

7 Marc Gutman, 'PPT Is DEAD. Why Bezos and Pichai Are Ditching the Deck for Storytelling...', 18 June 2017. https://www.linkedin.com/ pulse/ppt-dead-why-bezos-pichai-ditching-deck-storytelling-marc- gutman

8 Frank Hedler. 'PowerPoint Is Dead', *Research Live*, 22 July 2016. http://www.research-live.com/article/opinion/ditch-the- powerpoint-and-build-the-data-product/id/5010002

10: Multitasking Is to Be Always Avoided

1 Travis Bradberry. 'Multitasking Damages Your Brain and Career, New Studies Suggest', *Forbes*, 8 October 2014. https://www.forbes.com/ sites/travisbradberry/2014/10/08/multitasking-damages-your- brain-and-career-new-studies-suggest/

2 Christian P. Janssen, Sandy J. Gould, Simon Y. Li, Duncan P. Brumby and Anna L. Cox. 'Integrating Knowledge of Multitasking and Interruptions across Different Perspectives and Research Methods', *International Journal of Human-Computer Studies* 79, (2015): 1-5. https://doi.org/10.1016/j.ijhcs.2015.03.002

3 'Brain Scans Reveal "gray matter" Differences in Media Multitaskers', *EurekAlert!*, 24 September 2014. https://www.eurekalert.org/news-releases/467495

4 Ashok Soota and S. R. Gopalan, *Entrepreneurship Simplified: From Idea to IPO*. India: Penguin, 2016.

5 Nandan Nilekani and Tanuj Bhojwani, *The Art of Bitfulness*. India: Penguin Random House, 2022.

6 Madeline Pace. 'A Benefit of Multitasking', *The Well*, 5 October 2020. https://thewell.unc.edu/2020/10/05/need-a-creativity-boost/

7 Chaitali Kapadia and Shimul Melwani, 'More Tasks, More Ideas: The Positive Spillover Effects of Multitasking on Subsequent Creativity', *Journal of Applied Psychology*, 106 (4), 2020. 10.1037/apl0000506

Part 3: Busting Myths about People and Organizations

11: We Are Under-Led and Over-Managed/Over-Led and Under-Managed

1 Next Generation, 'The Difference between Leadership and Management', https://www.nextgeneration.ie/blog/2018/03/the-difference-between-leadership-and-management?source=google.com

2 Jeremiah Sinks, 'Organizations Are Over-Managed and Under-Led', Purdue University, 1 September 2019. https://mep.purdue.edu/news-folder/organizations-are-over-managed-and-under-led/

3 Brigette Hyacinth, 'Leadership or Management. Which Is More Important?', 30 June 2017. https://www.linkedin.com/pulse/leadership-management-which-more-important-brigette-hyacinth

4 Henry Mintzberg, *Simply Managing: What Managers Do—and Can Do Better*. United Kingdom: Pearson, 2013.

5 Henry Mintzberg, 'The Best Leadership Is Good Management', *The Economic Times*, 11 August 2009. https://economictimes. indiatimes.com/the-best-leadership-is-good-management/articleshow/4881300.cms?from=mdr

6 Randy Mayeux. 'Which Is It? Overmanaged and Underled—or, Undermanaged and Overled? How about Undermanaged and Underled?', *First Friday Book Synopsis*, 9 August 2009. https://ffbsccn.wordpress. com/2009/08/09/which-is-it-over managed-and-underled-or-undermanaged-and-overled-or-undermanaged-and-underled/

7 Ross Ashcroft. 'Over Managed and Under Led', 14 March 2016. https://www.linkedin.com/pulse/over-managed-under-led-ross-ashcroft

8 Troy Segal, 'Enron Scandal: The Fall of a Wall Street Darling', *Investopedia*, 5 April 2023. https://www.investopedia.com/updates/enron-scandal-summary/

9 Ashok Panigrahi, Antra Sinha, Anshul Garg and Astha Mehta, 2019, 'A Case Study on the Downfall of Kingfisher Airlines', *Journal of Management Research and Analysis*, 6: 81–84, 10.18231/j.jmra.2019.014.

10 Nicholas Thompson, 'Why Steve Ballmer Failed', *The New Yorker*, 23 August 2013. https://www.newyorker.com/business/currency/why-steve-ballmer-failed

11 Rockwell, Dan. 'Over-Led and Under-Managed', *Leadership Freak*, 27 April 2016. https://leadershipfreak.blog/2016/04/27/over-led-and-under-managed/

12: We Can Train People to Become Leaders

1 'Size of the Training Industry', *Training Industry*, 29 March 2021. https://trainingindustry.com/wiki/learning-services-and-outsourcing/size-of-training-industry/

2 Technavio. 'The Corporate Leadership Training Market Size to Grow by USD 15.78 Billion | Market Insights Highlights the Increased Spending on Corporate Leadership as Key Driver', *PR Newswire*, 11 January 2022. https://www.prnewswire.com/news-releases/the-corporate-leadership-training-market-size-to-grow-by-usd-15-78-billion--market-insights-highlights-the-increased-spending-on-corporate-leadership-as-key-driver--technavio-301457106.html

3 Michael Beer, Magnus Finnström and Derek Schrader. 'Why Leadership Training Fails—and What to Do about It', *Harvard Business Review*, 1 October 2016. https://hbr.org/2016/10/why-leadership- training-fails-and-what-to-do-about-it

4 'Is Leadership Learned or Innate?', *The Success Factory*. https://www.thesuccessfactory.co.uk/blog/is-leadership-learned-or-innate

5 Victor Lipman. *The Type B Manager: Leading Successfully in a Type A World*. United States: Penguin, 2015.

13: Empowerment Is about Authority to Make Decisions

1 Scott E. Seibert, Gang Wang and Stephen H. Courtright, 'Antecedents and Consequences of Psychological and Team Empowerment in Organizations: A Meta-Analytic Review', *The Journal of Applied*

Psychology 96, no. 5 (September 2011): 981–1003. https://doi.org/10.1037/a0022676

2 Mady Peterson, 'Employee Empowerment in the Workplace: 6 Steps to Take Today', *Limeade*, 11 April 2018. https://www.limeade.com/resources/blog/importance-of-employee-empowerment-in-the-workplace/

3 Daniel Brosseau, Sherina Ebrahim, Christina Handscomb and Shail Thaker. 'The Journey to an Agile Organization', McKinsey & Company. https://www.mckinsey.com/capabilities/people-and-organizational- performance/our-insights/the-journey-to-an-agile-organization

4 'Five Tips to Write an Effective Job Advertisement in Vietnam', *Agile Vietnam*, 1 April 2014. https://agilevietnam.com/

5 Bernard Marr, 'Why Empowering Employees to Make Decisions Is More Important Than Ever', *Forbes*, 5 May 2020. https://www.forbes.com/sites/bernardmarr/2020/05/05/why-empowering-employees-to-make-decisions-is-more-important-than-ever/

6 Aaron De Smet, Caitlin Hewes and Leigh Weiss. 'For Smarter Decisions, Empower Your Employees', McKinsey & Company. https://www.mckinsey.com/capabilities/people-and-organizational-performance/our-insights/for-smarter-decisions-empower-your-employees

7 Susan M. Heithfield, 'Boost Your Business by Empowering Employees to Think and Act', *LiveAbout*, 18 July 2019. https://www.liveabout.com/empowerment-in-action-how-to-empower-your-employees-1918102

8 Gustavo Razzetti, 'People Don't Need to Be Empowered (They Want This Instead)', *Fearless Culture*, 12 January 2021. https://fearlessculture.design/blog-posts/people-dont-need-to-be-empowered-they-want-this-instead

9 Allan Lee, Sara Willis and Amy Wei Tian. 'When Empowering Employees Works, and When It Doesn't', *Harvard Business Review*, 2 March 2018. https://hbr.org/2018/03/when-empowering- employees-works-and-when-it-doesnt

14: People Resist Change

1 Paul R. Lawrence, 'How to Deal with Resistance to Change', *Harvard Business Review*, 1 January 1969. https://hbr.org/1969/01/how-to-deal-with-resistance-to-change

2 Robert Tanner, 'Organizational Change: 8 Reasons Why People Resist Change', *Management Is a Journey*, 28 January 2023. https://

managementisajourney.com/organizational-change-8-reasons-why-people-resist-change/

3 Jim Collins and James Charles Collins, *Good to Great: Why Some Companies Make the Leap ... and Others Don't.* United Kingdom: Random House, 2001.

4 Jonathan Mills, 'Appoint Early Adopters as Change Champions', Stretch for Growth, 14 July 2019. https://www.stretchforgrowth.com/organisational-effectiveness/appoint-early-adopters-as-change-champions/

5 Sandhya Mendonca and T.T.K. Jagannathan, *Disrupt and Conquer: How TTK Prestige Became a Billion-Dollar Business.* India: Penguin Random House, 2018.

15: Firing the Bottom 10 Per Cent

1 Julie Bort, 'This Is Why Some Microsoft Employees Still Fear the Controversial "Stack Ranking" Employee Review System', *Business Insider*, 27 August 2014. https://www.businessinsider.in/this-is-why-some-microsoft-employees-still-fear-the-controversial-stack-ranking-employee-review-system/articleshow/41022639.cms

2 David Gelles, *The Man Who Broke Capitalism: How Jack Welch Gutted the Heartland and Crushed the Soul of Corporate America—and How to Undo His Legacy.* United Kingdom: Simon & Schuster, 2022.

3 Malcolm Gladwell, 'Was Jack Welch the Greatest C.E.O. of His Day—or the Worst?', *The New Yorker*, 31 October 2022. https://www.newyorker.com/magazine/2022/11/07/was-jack-welch-the-greatest-ceo-of-his-day-or-the-worst

4 Carla Tardi, 'The 80-20 Rule (aka Pareto Principle): What It Is, How It Works', *Investopedia*, 7 March 2023. https://www.investopedia.com/ terms/1/80-20-rule.asp

5 'Pareto Principle (80/20 rule) and Pareto Analysis Guide,' *Juran*, 12 March 2019. https://www.juran.com/blog/a-guide-to-the-pareto-principle-80-20-rule-pareto-analysis/

6 Anna Verasai, 'What Up or Out Policy Means to Workers', *The HR Digest*, 12 September, 2019. https://www.thehrdigest.com/what-up-or-out-policy-means-to-workers/

7 Paul B. Brown, 'Should You Fire 10% of Your Employees Every Year?', Inc.com, 17 July, 2014. https://www.inc.com/paul-b-brown/should- you-fire-10-of-your-employees-every-year.html

8 Marc Effron, 'Why You Need to Fire the Next 10 Percent', *TalentQ*, 15 October 2021. https://www.talent-quarterly.com/why-you-need-to-fire-the-next-10-percent/

16: People Leave People, Not Organizations

1 Greg Rosalsky, 'Why Are So Many Americans Quitting Their Jobs?', *NPR*, 19 October 2021, Newsletter Section. https://www.npr.org/sections/money/2021/10/19/1047032996/why-are-so-many-americans-quitting-their-jobs; Brigette Hyacinth, 'Employees Don't Quit Their Job; They Quit Their Boss!', 23 February 2021. https://brigettehyacinth.com/employees-dont-quit-their-job- they-quit-their-boss/
2 'Great Places to Work Inc', a global entity that assesses organizations on culture and whether they qualify as great places to work.
3 Didier Elzinga, 'The Biggest Lie in HR: People Quit Bosses Not Companies', *Culture Amp*. https://www.cultureamp.com/blog/biggest-lie-people-quit-bosses
4 Greg Rosalsky, 'Why Are So Many Americans Quitting Their Jobs?', 19 October 2021, *NPR*, https://www.npr.org/sections/money/2021/10/19/1047032996/why-are-so-many-americans-quitting-their-jobs#:~:text=But%20the%20historic%20rise%20in,our%20lives%20and%20the%20world.
5 Prasanna Mohanty, 'Indian Economy's Great Dichotomy: Labour Shortage amidst Job Losses!', *Fortune*, 7 April 2022. https:// www.fortuneindia.com/opinion/indian-economys-great-dichotomy-labour-shortage-amidst-job-losses/107979
6 Lohit Bhatia, 'The Great Resignation Is Hurting IT Sector the Most', 15 May 2022, https://www.deccanherald.com/business/business-news/the-great-resignation-is-hurting-it-sector-the-most-lohit-bhatia-1109528.html
7 Namanhr.com, 'The Great Resignation Survey 2022', https:// www.namanhr.com/wp-content/uploads/2022/06/the_g reat_ resignation_survey_2022_final_1.pdf

17: You Should Hire People Smarter Than Yourself

1 Leveling Up, 'Should You Hire People That are Smarter Than You? A Data-Driven Answer', https://www.levelingup.com/hiring/should-you-hire-people-that-are-smarter-than-you-a-data-driven-answer/

2 Mishra, Bibhu Ranjan. 'Ashok Soota's second act', Business Standard, 21 January 2013, Features Section. https://www.business-standard.com/article/companies/ashok-soota-s-second-act-111091400032_1.html

3 Dunning-Kruger effect, in psychology, is a cognitive bias whereby people with limited knowledge or competence in a given intellectual or social domain greatly overestimate their knowledge or competence in that domain, relative to objective criteria or the performance of their peers or of people in general.

Index

About the Authors

Ashok Soota is the founding chairman of Happiest Minds Technologies and was the founding chairman of MindTree.

Peter de Jager is an internationally known keynote speaker, writer and consultant on change management.

About the Coauthor

Sandhya Mendonca is the founder and managing director of Raintree Media, and an author.

For updates on workshops and news related to *Busted*, follow https://www.petrusdejager.com/

Harper
Collins

4th

HARPER
PERENNIAL

HARPER
BUSINESS

HARPER
BLACK

हार्पर
हिन्दी

HarperCollins
Children'sBooks

HARPER
DESIGN

HARPER
VANTAGE

Harper
Sport